ORBITA
THE PROJECT

arcpublications.co.uk/orbita

This book is accompanied by a dedicated website, showcasing selected works by ORBITA *which we are unable to reproduce in print.*

*Throughout the book, you will see Quick Response (*QR*) codes, which look like this:*

When scanned with the camera on your smart phone or tablet, these codes will take you directly to an item on the website.

(If you do not have one of these devices, you can simply type the web address at the top of this page into your normal internet browser.)

If you are using an Apple device (iPhone, iPad, iPod) running iOS 11 or later, simply open the camera app and point the camera at the QR *code. A notification will appear at the top of the screen – tap this to go straight to the website.*

If you are using an earlier version of iOS, or an Android device, you will need to install an app to read QR *codes. Simply search the App Store or the Play Store for "*QR *code reader" and choose the one you prefer.*

You can try it out by scanning the QR *code above, which will take you to the homepage of the website accompanying this book.*

ORBITA
О Р Б И Т А
THE PROJECT
П Р О Е К Т

Poems by
Semyon Khanin
Sergej Timofejev
Vladimir Svetlov
Artūrs Punte

Translated by
Kevin M. F. Platt
with
Polina Barskova, Charles Bernstein, Julia Bloch,
Daniil Cherkassky, Sarah Dowling, Natalia Fedorova,
Eugene Ostashevsky, Karina Sotnik, Sasha Spektor,
Anton Tenser, Maya Vinokour
Michael Wachtel and Matvei Yankelevich

Preface by Tony Ward
Introduction by Steven J. Fowler
Edited by Jean Boase-Beier

2018

Published by Arc Publications
Nanholme Mill, Shaw Wood Road
Todmorden, OL14 6DA, UK
www.arcpublications.co.uk

Copyright in the poems © individual poets as named, 2018
Copyright in the translations © Kevin M. F. Platt &
other translators as named, 2018
Copyright in the Preface © Tony Ward 2018
Copyright in the Introduction © S J Fowler 2018
Copyright in the present edition © Arc Publications Ltd, 2018

Printed by
Lightning Source

978 1911469 32 2 (pbk)
978 1911469 33 9 (ebk)

ACKNOWLEDGEMENTS

The following poems from the collection *Hit Parade* (Ugly Duckling Presse, 2015) are reprinted by permission of UDP and Kevin M. F. Platt: SEMYON KHANIN's 'lips groping for the mouths,' 'do not think he is homeless,' 'why did I keep yelling I'm an electrician,' 'when in a spacesuit of highly sensitive skin,' 'some virgins concealing…,'; VLADIMIR SVETLOV's 'on aveņu avenue,' 'from this our tenderness,' 'what'll you say?' 'let's depart for where they caught us' 'The Beautiful,' 'say "raisin," baby,' 'Confidential Conversation,' 'Hit Parade,' 'Money,' 'Empty Airport,'; ARTŪRS PUNTE's 'She prepared well,' 'Peculiar things are at times fastened,' 'Where were you led by the keyword search,' 'Metatarsal, tarsal, phalanges of the digits,' 'A Year's Time,' 'It happened that a girl from Dzhokar…,'.

The publishers wish to thank the editors of the following magazines in which some of these poems have appeared: *Common Knowledge*, *World Literature Today*, *Poem*, and *Supplement*.

They would also like to express their gratitude to Inga Bodnarjuka, and the Latvian Literature Centre, without whose help this project would not have been possible.

Arc Publications is grateful to the Latvian Ministry of Culture and the Latvian Writers Union for their financial support of this project.

This book is copyright. Subject to statutory exception and to provisions of relevant collective licensing agreements, no reproduction of any part of this book may take place without the written permission of Arc Publications Limited.

**Arc Publications 'Anthologies in Translation'
Series Editor: Jean Boase-Beier**

CONTENTS

About Orbita / 7
About the Translation / 9
Preface / 11
Introduction / 13

SEMYON KHANIN

17 / at the bus station…	нарисуется на автовокзале / 91
18 / lips groping for the mouths…	нащупывая губами горлышко / 92
19 / let me tell you a story…	вот такая история… / 93
20 / I was riding my bike…	я ехал на велике… / 94
21 / it's kind of dumb to say goodbye in advance…	как-то глупо прощаться заранее / 95
22 / bronze-faced statue…	бронзоволицая статуя / 96
23 / overpurred to senselessness…	замурлыканный до бесчувствия… / 97
24 / you fear and anticipate, when will it come…	и боишься, и ждешь, когда он наступит / 98
26 / quickly quickly pull it out of your pocket…	быстро-быстро вынь из кармана… / 100
27 / standing at the edge…	стоя на краю могилы… / 101
28 / do not think he is homeless…	не подумай, что это бездомный / 102
29 / why did I keep yelling I'm an electrician…	зачем я так кричал, что я электрик / 103
30 / when in a spacesuit of highly sensitive skin…	когда в скафандре из очень чувствительной кожи / 104
31 / some virgins concealing …	какие-то девы, скрывавшие… / 105

SERGEJ TIMOFEJEV

35 / Morning in a Land of Introverts	Утро в стране интровертов / 109
36 / Quiet God	Тихий Бог / 110
39 / Her Oil	Её нефть / 113
40 / The System in the System	Система в системе / 114
42 / Bugs, Boughs	Жучки, веточки / 116
43 / Forecast	Прогноз / 117
44 / Barefoot	Босиком / 118
45 / Popular Song for Ukulele	Популярная мелодия для укулеле / 119
46 / Something Like a Report	Что-то вроде доклада / 120
47 / The Ritz	Отель Ритц / 121
49 / Postcommunication	Посткоммуникация / 123
50 / Figures of Speech	Фигуры речи / 124
51 / Questions	Вопросы / 125
52 / Field Trips	Экскурсии / 126

VLADIMIR SVETLOV

55 / on aveņu avenue… • на aveņu авеню / 129
56 / from this our tenderness… • от этой нашей нежности / 130
57 / what'll you say?… • что скажешь? / 131
58 / lets depart for where they caught us… • давай уйдем туда, где нас застали / 132
59 / The Beautiful • Красивое / 133
60 / Say "raisin," baby… • скажи «изюм» детка / 134
61 / Confidential Conversation • Конфиденциальный разговор / 135
62 / Click, Click • Клик, клик / 136
63 / Hit Parade • Хит-парад / 137
64 / Money • Деньги / 138
65 / Empty Airport • Пустой аэропорт / 139
66 / Classmate • Одноклассник / 140

ARTŪRS PUNTE

71 / The path to his stone on the high dune… • Дорожка к его камню на высокой дюне / 145
72 / The Rule of Mnemonics • Мнемоническое правило / 146
74 / Highway • Шоссе / 148
75 / Through the rustle of the earth works… • Сквозь шелест земляных работ / 149
76 / One-and-a-halfth Floor • Полторой этаж / 150
77 / Trip to the City • Поездка в город / 151
78 / Today I understood… • Сегодня я понял / 152
79 / Wrong Season • Не сезон / 153
80 / Now Hiring • Требуются / 154
81 / She prepared well… • Она хорошо подготовилась / 155
82 / Peculiar things are at times fastened… • Странные вещи бывают порой прикреплены / 156
83 / Where were you led by the keyword search… • Куда завел по ключевому слову поиск / 157
84 / Metatarsal, tarsal, phalanges of the digits… • Предплюсна, плюсна, фаланги пальцев / 158
85 / A Year's Time • Год времени / 159
86 / It happened that a girl from Dzhokhar… • Как-то полюбила меня девушка с улицы Джохара Дудаева / 160

Biographical Notes / 163

ABOUT ORBITA

PHOTO: TOMS HARJO

Artūrs Punte   Semyon Khanin   Sergej Timofejev   Vladimir Svetlov

ORBITA is a creative collective / group of Latvian poets writing in Russian whose works are dedicated to dialogue between various creative genres (literature, music, video, photography, VJ, web, etc.) and cultures. The collective was founded 1999 in Riga. Since that time ORBITA has published a number of eponymously-titled almanacs in which literary works appear side by side with works of visual art (photography, graphic work, painting). Additionally, ORBITA has organized five "Word in Motion" festivals of poetry, video and multi-media art in Latvia (in 2001, 2003, 2007, 2009 and 2011); issued two poetry CDs and a collection of poetry videos; created several multi-media poetry installations for public exhibition; produced a number of bilingual (Russian-Latvian) poetry collections and publications; issued an anthology of contemporary Russian poetry in Latvia; and published a number of other works.

ORBITA actively participates in Latvian and international cultural life. Members of the group have been published in many European countries and are frequently invited to literary and artistic festivals in Germany, Russia, Italy, Finland, Spain, Croatia, Estonia, Lithuania, Belarus, Ukraine, Switzerland and Sweden. In 2015 their installation *Two sonnets from Laputa* was included in the

Venice Biennial Collateral events programme.

In November 2016 the ORBITA poets went on a 10-day tour in the USA, performing in New York, Washington, Philadelphia and Yale to present their poetry collection Hit Parade, published in the USA by Ugly Duckling Presse. Poems by Orbita poets have appeared, or are forthcoming, in the magazines Common Knowledge, World Literature Today, Poem and Supplement.

In Latvia, ORBITA's achievements have been recognized with the Annual Literary Prize of the Union of Latvian Writers, the Annual Prize for the best photography album and the best photography exhibit, as well as a number of prizes for book design, poetry video and various other literary and artistic awards.

Since its inception, ORBITA has appeared in literary and multimedia performances in conjunction with invited musicians and video-artists. During recent years the artistic development of the group has also gone in the direction of synergy of poetry and the visual arts, technologies, perception of poetry, sound and performance art.

ABOUT THE TRANSLATION

The poems included in this volume have been carried out in various contexts and by various translators over the past decade. Most of them have been, in one way or another, collaborative translation projects. Some of the earliest translations included here were completed at the first Your Language My Ear symposium at the University of Pennsylvania's Kelly Writers House in 2011—this is a recurrent event that involves a combination of virtual collaboration followed by intensive workshopping of the resulting draft translations in small groups. The participants of the 2011 gathering included the poets, translators and scholars Polina Barskova, Charles Bernstein, Julia Bloch, Evgeny Ostashevsky, Maya Vinokour, Michael Wachtel, and Matvei Yankelevich.

Other poems included here were translated by the team of Anton Tenser, Sasha Spektor, and Daniil Cherkassky in the context of the Chicago Translation Workshop. Still others are collaborations between Karina Sotnik and myself, working in close proximity, or between the new media poet and scholar Natalia Fedorova and myself, linked only through virtual channels. Finally, even those poems that I carried out ostensibly "alone" were executed in close consultation with the poets of ORBITA, who have a great deal to contribute to discussions of translation practices, given how frequently they translate into Russian themselves. This is, of course, a reflection of the special position of the ORBITA poets in Latvia's multilingual society and literary community.

In general, the translators have strived to render the lexical choices and tonality of the original poems with a great deal of fidelity, while also working to carry over, insofar as possible, the rhythmic construction, occasional deployments of rhyme and other phonic effects, and wordplay (in particular, inter-linguistic Latvian-Russian wordplay, as in Vladimir Svetlov's "on aveņu avenue"). A few of the poems translated at Your Language My Ear depart to some degree from this rule, taking more liberties with the choices of the original poets, in a reflection of the democratic and experimental principles of that gathering.

In what follows, if no translator is credited for a given poem, then I carried out its translation alone. Otherwise, the names of translators are listed at the conclusion of respective poems.

Kevin M. F. Platt

VLADIMIR SVETLOV

55 / on avenu avenue… • на avenu авеню / 129
56 / from this our tenderness… • от этой нашей нежности / 130
57 / what'll you say?… • что скажешь? / 131
58 / lets depart for where they caught us… • давай уйдем туда, где нас застали / 132
59 / The Beautiful • Красивое / 133
60 / Say "raisin," baby… • скажи «изюм» детка / 134
61 / Confidential Conversation • Конфиденциальный разговор / 135
62 / Click, Click • Клик, клик / 136
63 / Hit Parade • Хит-парад / 137
64 / Money • Деньги / 138
65 / Empty Airport • Пустой аэропорт / 139
66 / Classmate • Одноклассник / 140

ARTŪRS PUNTE

71 / The path to his stone on the high dune… • Дорожка к его камню на высокой дюне / 145
72 / The Rule of Mnemonics • Мнемоническое правило / 146
74 / Highway • Шоссе / 148
75 / Through the rustle of the earth works… • Сквозь шелест земельных работ / 149
76 / One-and-a-halfth Floor • Полторой этаж / 150
77 / Trip to the City • Поездка в город / 151
78 / Today I understood… • Сегодня я понял / 152
79 / Wrong Season • Не сезон / 153
80 / Now Hiring • Требуются / 154
81 / She prepared well… • Она хорошо подготовилась / 155
82 / Peculiar things are at times fastened… • Странные вещи бывают порой прикреплены / 156
83 / Where were you led by the keyword search… • Куда завел по ключевому слову поиск / 157
84 / Metatarsal, tarsal, phalanges of the digits… • Предплюсна, плюсна, фаланги пальцев / 158
85 / A Year's Time • Год времени / 159
86 / It happened that a girl from Dzhokhar… • Как-то полюбила меня девушка с улицы Джохара Дудаева / 160

Biographical Notes / 163

CONTENTS

About Orbita / 7
About the Translation / 9
Preface / 11
Introduction / 13

SEMYON KHANIN

17 / at the bus station… • нарисуется на автовокзале / 91
18 / lips groping for the mouths… • нащупывая губами горлышко / 92
19 / let me tell you a story… • вот такая история… / 93
20 / I was riding my bike… • я ехал на велике… / 94
21 / it's kind of dumb to say goodbye in advance… • как-то глупо прощаться заранее / 95
22 / bronze-faced statue… • бронзоволицая статуя / 96
23 / overpurred to senselessness… • замурлыканный до бесчувствия… / 97
24 / you fear and anticipate, when will it come… • и боишься, и ждешь, когда он наступит / 98
26 / quickly quickly pull it out of your pocket… • быстро-быстро вынь из кармана… / 100
27 / standing at the edge… • стоя на краю могилы… / 101
28 / do not think he is homeless… • не подумай, что это бездомный / 102
29 / why did I keep yelling I'm an electrician… • зачем я так кричал, что я электрик / 103
30 / when in a spacesuit of highly sensitive skin… • когда в скафандре из очень чувствительной кожи / 104
31 / some virgins concealing … • какие-то девы, скрывавшие… / 105

SERGEJ TIMOFEJEV

35 / Morning in a Land of Introverts • Утро в стране интровертов / 109
36 / Quiet God • Тихий Бог / 110
39 / Her Oil • Её нефть / 113
40 / The System in the System • Система в системе / 114
42 / Bugs, Boughs • Жучки, веточки / 116
43 / Forecast • Прогноз / 117
44 / Barefoot • Босиком / 118
45 / Popular Song for Ukulele • Популярная мелодия для укулеле / 119
46 / Something Like a Report • Что-то вроде доклада / 120
47 / The Ritz • Отель Ритц / 121
49 / Postcommunication • Посткоммуникация / 123
50 / Figures of Speech • Фигуры речи / 124
51 / Questions • Вопросы / 125
52 / Field Trips • Экскурсии / 126

PREFACE

In 1968, when the politics of Europe were near boiling point, when there were demonstrations across the world against the Vietnam War, when students demonstrated *en masse* against the excesses of capitalism, it was the arts that reflected these momentous events and political movements. Particularly active at this turbulent time in Europe were poetic movements, with both Right and Left vying for attention. In the UK, the hugely influential mid-Atlantic movement introduced, through the output of the Black Mountain School, a different and exciting poetic, an element of which was 'concrete' poetry. The term 'concrete' was deliberately non-specific, thus allowing the existence of many different ideas, interpretations and political perspectives, all of which were considered valid. (Unlike the small presses, the mainstream publishers at this time would have nothing to do with the mid-Atlantic movement, preferring to maintain a genteel and uncontroversial approach to publishing.) The concrete movement in the UK was firmly based on language, visual interpretation and the voice, and it developed in three different ways, largely determined by the three geographical regions from which its main exponents came.

The Gloucester Movement consisted of artists such as Dom Sylvester Houédard and John Furnival. Their work, which was made up of words, letters and alphabets, was highly visual. Furnival, whose work was firmly based in the English language, made extremely clever, frequently overtly political, pictures using letters. Houédard used only his typewriter, committing his work to the page via letters or phrases in varieties of patterns and colours. The Westminster Group had two very fine exponents, Bob Cobbing and Bill Griffiths. They used language, letters, typewriters and illustrative motifs to show the relationship between hard copy and performance. They were brilliant at making perfect sense of what appeared a totally random text on a page. The third group was the Scottish group headed by Ian Hamilton Finlay. This group was distinguished by its use of different media – neon signs, embroidery, differing typefaces, sculptures and printed text – to demonstrate how language could be used, transformed and translated to arrive at different interpretations. This period was hugely exciting as concrete poetry opened up, for everyone, a way not only into literature but into art in its broadest sense. It also shaped political policy (for example, school teaching methods), architectural practice and it fostered a general tolerance of things new, unexpected and, at first glance, incomprehensible.

This state of affairs was not to last. Old age took its toll and the political circumstances changed when, in 1979, Margaret Thatcher demolished the *status quo* in favour of more oppressive right-wing elements in order to maintain a grip on power. Any movements that were openly questioning policy or advocating progress, particularly within English progressive education, were quickly disabled. Thus, slowly but surely, the arts in general, and poetry in particular, suffered a retrenchment to the 'old values' that celebrated conservatism in all its guises.

For many years, the ethos of 'concrete' was largely forgotten, or at least sidelined, in the UK. A few exponents still practise and try to make a footprint, but alas, to very little effect, their work being almost totally ignored or consigned to the museums or galleries.

Imagine my surprise, therefore, on a visit to Latvia in 2016 at being introduced to a group of poets calling themselves ORBITA, a group of Russian-speaking Latvian citizens who have, without knowing it, continued the ideas of the UK 'concrete' of the 1960s and 70s. They are practising forms of poetics which range from the more conservative written language to experimental work that the UK poets of half a century ago dreamed of but never achieved. This small group of dedicated poets, all firmly committed to using language itself, and poetry in particular, to introduce pure performance – be it visual, sound, sculpture or film – have established themselves as a small but vital part of Latvian culture. It has to be said that their interpretation of performance is far removed from the 'performance poetry' that has taken hold in the UK (reminiscent of that practised by the 'new wave' of the late 1950s): ORBITA's methods are unique in as much as *nothing* need be excluded, which makes their principles and objectives all the more exciting and unpredictable.

Join 'concrete' with Fluxus and you will have an idea of ORBITA, of what it has achieved and what it could achieve in the future. ORBITA allows the discipline of a native tongue to range across a universal canvas and be translated, celebrated, explored, enjoyed and developed by all.

Tony Ward

INTRODUCTION

The possibilities of poetry will not disappear. The content and the context of a poem will change to its times, shaped by its authors, visible or otherwise, but the actual potential of poetry, is not contingent on political vagaries or cultural changes, even if they are seismic. And even if they are fascinating to a British reader of poetry, who, and I mean this without accusation, will perhaps be more excited by a fetishized personal detail marking the life of a poet, than the poetry they have written. It is tempting then to remark upon Latvia's recent history, it's nascent national identity out of the shadow forest of the Soviet Union and what this means for our understanding of ORBITA, given the fact they are Russian language poets. Yet what I would like to say is that the possibilities of poetry will not disappear and if they stand for something, in light of recent history, it is this.

There is a bond between those who have recognised innovation is required in the face of a changing world if one is just going to be contemporary, let alone future facing. ORBITA, in Latvia, have created space where no space existed before. Beyond Latvia, they have recognised that before sound poetry there was an endless ubiquitous human practise of non-semantic vocal art, so sound poetry is essential. That before concrete poetry there were the multifarious religious and secular traditions of writing art whose shape contained as much meaning as its words, so it is permanent. That the modern era is the technological era, that humans might record, trap and relocate their voices for the first time ever and share their works on the page at speed, in great numbers. That there has been unending changes to our very existence and the language that mediates it. And so, the possibilities of poetry will not only not dissipate, but scream out at poets, that they must answer this change, or drive their heads into the sand, looking back, over their shoulders, to a time when poetry might be allusive in order not to bring down physical oppression, or even further, when formalism was a way of negotiating a metaphysical drive. What ORBITA have done, in my eyes, is be alive to this potential, with extraordinary energy, originality, power and innovation. They have done this through a range of methodologies which seem organic to their work, that seem all the more remarkable because they have been so consistent, prolific and ever evolving, and have done this with a longevity few avant garde collectives can maintain.

They have been alive to their nation, to its traditions, to its rapidly changing character, and they have marked this in their work, presenting an aberrant history of sorts, as they are alive to the Russian language and to unmissable Western influences. Their poetry can be visual, cinematic, sonic, collaborative, theatrical, but this agility and adaptability never detracts from what they do upon the page, having written poems that are powerfully imagistic, often colloquial, rhythmic, semantically complex and clever.

It is no exaggeration to declare ORBITA as one of the most adventurous poetic collectives in the recent history of Europe, beyond the Baltic. They have been, singularly, a fundamental part of the radical reconfiguration of their nation's poetic culture and landscape in the last few decades and it is to Latvia's credit that this has been recognised. They emerge, urbane, grounded, naturalistic, with an output that has been marked by consistent innovation in a region many associate with formalism. This volume, I hope, stands as a testament to that, a moment for English language readers to reflect on what is possible and perhaps, what is most exciting in twenty-first century European poetry.

Steven J. Fowler

SEMYON KHANIN

* * *

at the bus station takes shape
a story a really old saw
a got-no-hackneyed tale
once upon a time a Chukchi, an Estonian, and an Old Jew
a German, Frenchman, and Russian in one person
met, a heart, liver, and a spleen
ran out of cash and from out of town
late for the bus no place to lay head
need a bit more to buy a ticket
if you can spare any extra then of course
go meet your relations at the station, she says
so up and went but it's been days and no sight
can't not demand a little loan, all in the family
one buck to spend the night in the waiting for nothing area
noisy trains can't really sleep
the canal splashing against foundations below
sit in the glassy café above the dispatcher's booth
after a glass or two the river comes in focus better
hear departures better maybe they'll announce the relations
seagulls fly in from the market pavilions
sensing bread and sausage in the buffet's depths
pocketbook found would owner please
proceed to information counter
grab at heart, at billfold
at crumpled self-portrait on ID
passport's stuck fast to the card
lost wallet has anyone found it
line shrinking at window six
a crowd again at the tram stop
where's the pan? info display burns bright
    for nothing
loudspeaker really hits hard
now boarding on platform number eight
climb into the freight compartment with the
    bags
head off to your native out of town
to meet with the one who sent you off
her song pouring from the well

* * *

lips groping for the mouths
of bottles cast into the sea
groping to drink their messages
mumbling through scribbles, obscure in places,
the guttural, whorled gurgle of bubbles

painstakingly articulating in polite formulas the crumpled
    beginnings

choking on wild laughter
to penetrate the details of the catastrophe

the ship sank
and the sun shrivelled up
and the capsized sea spilled out
and we're here
we're here
here

we, your surrogate brothers and sisters
related by reason, naturally – how else –
extraneous reason maybe, extraterrestrial maybe
does it make any difference at this degree of amnesia
for those who have tasted unearthly bliss

we, the very same gelatinous heavenly
    creatures
lost in the uninhabited reinforced
    concrete jungles
standing deathly contorted like
    undiscovered pseudorangutans
on the uncultivated coast of a longed-for
    Champansee
we're waiting for the signal and dying
    of thirst

here the ink became blurred
and through pink and blue jellyfish lenses
were seen the washed-out remains
    of flat impassive faces

Translated by Kevin M. F. Platt,
Julia Bloch & Maya Vinokour

* * *

let me tell you a story from when I was still a burglar
I plied my trade in the suburbs, cleaned out private residences
one time I wound up with this married couple; they were already sleeping
I was going through the bedroom, they were in this huge bed, him facing up
towards the ceiling and her flopped out in a nightie, and both
were talking in their sleep, so I stand there on my tip toes by the wall and he says:
"I don't believe you, your words are good for a couple of days, then they
turn into cardboard, lies…" then he wheezed through his nose. She was silent,
then sighed: "woven… right here and here… sitting in our box…"
"no matter," he seemed to reply, then hollowly "she's already here,"
and then she began to laugh, for real, in short spurts, but often and piercingly
"don't you touch me," her voice trembled, "don't dare." He snorted and I was
already getting ready to move on, when he clearly pronounced: "glass,
glass has frozen into the ice, shards, hide… hide me, I can't…
you're killing me," while she was saying at the same time: "there's no firing pin,
we don't have any, you might ask a collector…" and with the last word she seemingly
completely ran out of energy. To this episode I owe a handful of silver
jewellery and portcigars. I knew that behind every picture was a safe,
and behind all of the wallpaper were mirrors. It was just like that, dear friends,
just like that, respected gentlemen.

* * *

I was riding my bike, the one that got stolen afterwards
with my girlfriend, the one I broke up with a year later
along that street that got completely rebuilt
to that café – later on it simply closed

we were happily rattling off our thoughts and our legs

now there's a pizzeria where the café used to be
I even go there sometimes
and order a four-cheese pizza
they bring it to me and the knife strokes through the pizza
remind me of spokes on a wheel

just like that: bike spokes – knife strokes

but just now, when I was riding on my bike
with my sweet girlfriend
along that well-known street
to our favourite café
I didn't stop to think that with every push on the pedals
I was also driving the world into entropy and chaos

although the pizza wasn't bad at all

* * *

it's kind of dumb to say goodbye in advance
this eternity with small breaks
real fractures in fake marble
and did anyone even suggest mentioning the significant gaps
yet within these constraints space for doubt exists

is it worth it now or afterwards or much later
holding the pose damp tree by suspiciously white blank wall
to voice instinctively the glance sliding
                                      from still undeveloped Polaroid ceilings
from home-made swollen mirrors
losing its grip in the uneven marble light

THE BOOKS

* * *

bronze-faced statue
slave girl with ivory teeth
two days before the auction
became ill

contorted
joints aching
fractures throb in overly thin wrists
coral lip bitten, bloodied from pain

paralysed in fear, she stares
neck deadened from strain, numb
one limp arm has fallen insensibly
note crumpled in fist, now dropped

the experienced conservator
has cosied up to her, resetting
the dislodged marble backbone
whispers "don't be afraid, it'll crack a bit"
about to boil over, tears cool

he works over the spot
where a smear has dried and hardened
on whitened knuckles
makes a brush from his whiskers
cleans up chips, seams, underarms, instep and maker's mark

later she'll tremble
at the mallet's strike
and instinctively recoil
when her new owner clicks his tongue

* * *

overpurred to senselessness, to numbed earlobes
the polar oracle will get up today on the wrong side of the bed
spit out the balled up cheat-sheet and feed it to the shredder
lie on the concrete's cold to lace up a boot, position the
megaphone at his lips, repeating to himself: "let hair grow long"
"weasel out a vacation," "drain their ink away"

the ink loses colour from his hounding. today
even its permanence ain't forever. the cheat-sheet will plug the
    megaphone
have to explain things with hand-waving, instead of your voice
the pinkie you sprained in the last war will be ringing.
erratically waving his little gold-leafed hands
in the wake of trains of portents on a dead-end branch line,

a passer-bye, through his teeth, tosses off a sacramental goodbye.

so hand out once again promises and believe in them yourself

* * *

you fear and anticipate, when will it come –
that day, when you will at last understand
that the world stands not on the backs of elephants and whales
but of nervous little hamsters

and you'll find out that babylon
is located in the vērmanes garden
where maidens lay on cardboard pedestals
in elaborate wigs portraying lions

and the yawning abysses will shut their doors
and trolleybus number one will lower its poles
not holding hands, housekeepers
will head back from the matīsa market

and army reservists will go out on the playgrounds
legs unsteady on the rubber soft-top
to distinguish fully the red swings
from the green slide, from the yellow horsey

and the vases on the opera house façade
will fill up with southern fruits, still warm
and beavers will perceive in their own tails
maris liepa's splayed foot

and the waters of the daugava will turn turquoise
for the edification of their numberless tributaries
and heads on the french embassy
    will turn
to see smoke belching from the
    opera house smoke-stack

and a climber will break through the thorns to the uppermost cables
and the last taxi will pull out from the chomsky bar
and bernard will at last put on a hat and coat
and lāčplēsha street will run straight and flat

and an anchorite will wander into berga bazaar
rattling his suitcase wheels on the paving stones
and some meatheads will get a black eye
from the girls at the entrance to the splendid palace

and the vacated tenants will whisper
more than they ought in the ears of cheated depositors
how fountains gush from dark canals
how people arrive tanned from warm southern countries

and the boosters will wipe the smiles from their faces
mistaking yet another supermarket for the train station
and the frozen river will be run over by the train
and then run over again by number two

and the stars will rise out of freedom's hands
and from the chasms a sunny drizzle will pour
and you and I will lay together on the lawn beneath the gingko
and try to lie completely still

Translated by Kevin M. F. Platt

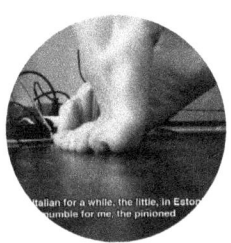

VIDEO: TALK WITH

* * *

quickly quickly pull it out of your pocket and put it in the glass
don't move, too soon, in general you shouldn't
and you –
stick out your tongue and squat
everything's OK, you were just going to the bar
move on, step along, step along
step on around
get your hand free, discreetly show your face
exhale so the lilac paint
smell comes out of your mouth
it's just you've held that cork so long it's nearly grown into your palm
but the ruins have been rebuilt, the wreckage is inhabited again
everything's OK, and there's already a replacement for you, too

VIDEO: ORCHESTRA REHEARSAL

* * *

standing at the edge of the grave, at the edge of all graves,
I address you in the name of all unstable elements,
in the name of the sidewound and shovelled-out and effaced,
in the name of the web-winged and defaced,
and in the name of all other faces, of faces of Caucasian origin,
and in the name of my own, wearisome to one and all, face,
and of all my other organs and body parts and universe,
I address you from the face and with the face,
address you insistently and at full voice
all you free shrubs and trees
all you creepy-crawlies, you dents, dimples and indentations,
all who still have the strength to hold their shrivelled little
                                                               weapons aloft,
all legumes
and the entire progressive heavenly vault and the horizon in particular:
friends! countrymen! ladies and gentlemen! little lapdogs!
at a moment when the entire world has eyes glued to binoculars,
when the hands of all humanity, of forest industry workers,
                                                of aunt Sonya,
            of all walleyes with a capital "w"
            and all lower case carp
            and all bream in small caps
are occupied with a single, all-important matter,
in this moment I address you with an appeal:
stand in even rows!
set legs shoulder-length apart!
put everything in place!
press your burning forehead against
    the night window!
and a-one, and a-two, and a-three,
    and a-four,
and a-one, and a-two, and a-three,
    and a-four!

* * *

do not think he is homeless
he simply lost his keys
and for the past four months he's been sleeping
in front of a furniture store

you might think he's uncomfortable
all doubled up like that
in fact he's an acrobat
and finds this posture handy for dozing

what makes you think he's dead
so what if he isn't breathing
what else do you expect from a yoga master
who can hold their breath for years at a time,

almost forever, to be exact

Translated by Anton Tenser, Sasha Spektor & Daniil Cherkassky

VIDEO: SVETA

* * *

why did I keep yelling I'm an electrician
I'm no electrician

what came over me

I gestured at outlets
cosied up to the circuit box, held the meter close

no one is buying it

here's my license, look, my certificate
wires sticking out of all my pockets

they just look at me in silence

give me five minutes and I'll close any circuit
I'll get soldering you won't be able to stop me

what kind of people are you

they shake their heads doubtfully
we can't use you, they say

we need an electrician

Translated by Kevin M. F. Platt, Julia Bloch, & Karina Sotnik

зачем я так кричал, что я электрик
ведь не электрик я

что на меня нашло

показывал руками на розетки
и льнул к щитку, и счетчик обнимал

никто не верит

вот справки, видите, вот документы
из всех карманов провода торчат

молчат и смотрят

да в пять минут замкну любые клеммы
не остановишь как начну паять

что вы за люди

качают головой с сомненьем
ты нам не нужен, говорят

нам бы электрика

* * *

when in a spacesuit of highly sensitive skin
in state of zero gravity
you lie motionless on the sofa
and everything within fogs up with your breathing
you shut your eyes you hear them singing
beyond the river, the gully, the forest
something like rusty sofa springs
and you wait for that thing:
that accompanied by an abrupt deep drag
the all-but-forgotten force of gravity enter your lungs

Translated by Eugene Ostashevsky

VIDEO: NEITHER TOMORROW NOR TODAY

* * *

some virgins concealing
their virginity – nurses? flight attendants, stewardesses? –
leaned over him, over the wounded veteran
whispering:
you are wounded, we wipe off your
blood.
and they would have
continued
wiping it if he hadn't resisted
in a most unnatural way
he died – in their care.
and they were not wiping him any more
but only his flesh
with their flashy useless dresses,
with their shawls unnecessary from that moment on

(sneakily
they savoured his image, unnatural)

(I wouldn't be surprised if he turned out to be
bulgarian like that
turgenev hero)

Translated by Sarah Dowling, Michael Wachtel & Polina Barskova

SERGEJ TIMOFEJEV

MORNING IN A LAND OF INTROVERTS

A dog softly barks
at a passing cyclist.
With restraint, the weather grows worse
and the barn falls apart.
Night birds are slightly critical
of the glories of the morning.
The sun can't remember
to what point it ascended yesterday
and aims slightly lower.
Children rise before everyone else
and read their books
trying not to wake the grown-ups.
Water pours modestly from the tap
not splashing and disappearing in the drain almost at once.
Shadows of firs and pines barely move.
Someone spreads butter in a thin layer on bread.
The Classics radio station airs an interview with a pianist
who answers every question with "yes" or "no".
Although he plays very precisely
with short, confident pauses.

УТРО В СТРАНЕ ИНТРОВЕРТОВ

Негромко лает собака
на проезжающего на велосипеде.
Сдержанно портится погода
и разрушается сарай.
Ночные птицы слегка критичны
по отношению к чудесам утра.
Солнце не может вспомнить,
до какой точки вчера всходило,
и старается взойти чуть ниже.
Дети просыпаются раньше всех
и читают свои книжки,
чтобы не будить взрослых.
Вода из крана льётся скромно,
не брызжет и почти сразу исчезает в стоке.
Еле еле движутся тени ёлок и сосен.
Кто-то намазывает бутерброд тонким слоем масла.
По радио «Классика» передают интервью пианиста,
который на всё отвечает: «да» или «нет».
Хотя играет он очень точно,
с небольшими уверенными паузами.

QUIET GOD

I don't really have time to think back about how I saw
The Quiet God, but if you want, I can tell you about it.
I mean – your programme's listeners…
We were driving home from a bash, a fair number of us, five people.
I was at the wheel; everyone else was asleep;

We'd been partying all night. There was this huge, cloudy morning
Everywhere all around. Puffy, coiling clouds were rushing
With some kind of new-found force, like vaporous animals who,
Seeing their master, were giving their all
In an effort to get close to him. Right above the road
Ahead, piercing the clouds, I saw
Steady streams of light. They fell to earth magnificently,
Like radiant ladders or the folds of glorious
Clothing. I stared in unwilling fascination, but being an experienced driver,
Braked and continued at lower speed, as though I was just out for a ride,
Coasting into this gloriousness. I felt like a billiard ball, suspended,
Ready to descend in another fraction of a second
Into a marvellous corner pocket. I gripped the wheel and smiled, I was
Ready to laugh, but soundlessly. The streams of light kept getting closer,
And I saw that I was about to drive right into them. Everything around,
Got a thousand times brighter, and I saw my fingers on the wheel,
Like never before in my life – they were half-transparent and you could see
The veins, bones and nerves, and they were also shining
From inside, like amber. And I screamed something, I don't remember what.
Everyone woke up in an instant, thinking it was an accident, and I screamed
And screamed – I couldn't stop, but managed to step on the brakes.
And my friends pulled me out of the driver's seat and lay me
On the ground, and slapped my face, and poured water on me
From a tubby plastic bottle, and asked: "What's
Wrong? WHAT's wrong?" And I couldn't answer and just
Pointed at the sky, from where, vertically and irreversibly,
God was descending, right on our heads. Then they
Finally saw it and started screaming too and ran off

In all directions, leaving me there on the ground. And the light finally
Became blinding, and everything around turned white.
And I couldn't distinguish anything any more, everything
Was the same colour, everything was just made of light, and I
Started crying, because I couldn't scream any longer,
And because there was such quietness all around. And in that
Moment the Quiet God spoke with me, and told me
Not to try jumping up and running away;
He said, "Rest!" And I felt the light touch my forehead
Like a hand. And I remembered being in my mother's tummy
And I curled up like that and lay there, while the light
Went through me, like the columns of some enormous, weightless
    temple.
And then it was all over and I keep laying there watching
As the light pulls away, departs, slowly and sadly. No, I
Didn't try to hold on or chase after it, but I was
So sad, like when you look and see that you've won
Twenty-five thousand in the lottery, and then you look closer,
And the ticket's from the last draw – in general, no go,
And you stand there with it in your hand and think, "Why?!"
And I stood there like that and thought, "Why?!" In about an hour

My friends found me again and without saying much
We got in the car and drove on. We got back to the city,
I drove everyone home, I got to my own place and went to bed.
Woke up in the morning; it was Monday; and I lay face down
On the pillow and waited, but nothing special was happening;
So I got up, showered and went to work. Now
Every weekend I drive back and forth along that road,
But I never see those clouds or that light. I can't say
That I've become a model Christian or anything else.
And there's no time to think about it anyway, with work up to here –
It's summer, height of the season. But when you invited me on the radio
I thought, OK, I'll go; maybe I'm not the only one,
Maybe I'll get a response from someone else
The light has gone through. Maybe then it would be a bit easier.
But I don't know what we'd talk about, and so maybe
We'd just be quiet together, would shake hands,
And then go our separate ways. So that's the story.
But if something like this happens to someone else,
Don't be afraid. And afterwards… write to me,
Please… The office has the address. Goodbye!

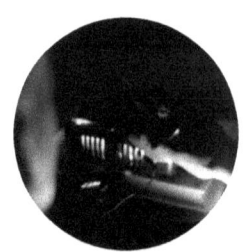

VIDEO: MAN & WOMAN

ТИХИЙ БОГ

Мне некогда вспоминать, как я у вял ал
Тихого bога, но если надо, я вам расскажу.
Я имею в виду – слушателям нашей программы.
Мы ехали с вечеринки, большой компанией, пять человек.
Я был за рулём, все остальные спали, перед этим
Провеселились всю ночь, было огромное облачное утро.
Поскольку, со всех сторон, пышные кучерявые облака плыли
С какой-то юной силой, как будто звероoбразные животные,
Заменившие своего хозяина и теперь шло от всех сил
Стремившиеся изобразиться в облаке. Прямо над дорогой
Впрерёд в уязвы пробивающиеся сквозь облака
Тонкие струи света, они падали вниз торжественно
Как лучистые лестницы или как следы великолепной
Оказии. Невольно я засмотрелся, но как опытный водитель
Сбросил скорости и ехал не спеша, будто просто катался
Вольфарный шар, готовый через долго секунды опуститься
Вытяжки и это великолепие. Я чувствовал себя как занятый
В гранёной лейкой. Я держал руль и улыбался, и был
Готов хохотать, но бесшумно. Струи света всё приближались,
И я понимал, что сейчас въеду прямо в них. Вокруг всё
Стало ярче в тысячу раз, и я увидел свои шпали на руке,
Как никогда в жизни, они стали полупрозрачными в них
Видны были жилки, косточки, нервы, они тоже светились.
Внутри, как янтарь. И я закрыл, и крикнул, что-то не помню что.
Всё произошло мгновенно, думал что авария. Я крикнул
И кринках – не моё остановиться, успел только запротестовать,
И мои спутники ветилыми меня из-за руля и повалили меня
На земле, и били меня по щекам, и лили на меня воду
Из пузатой пластиковой бутылки, и спрашивали: «Что
С тобой, ЧТО с тобой?» А я не мог ответить и только
Показывал на небо, откуда тихо спокойно и непоправимо
Спускался бог, прямо нам на головы. И тогда они
Наконец унтали и тоже закрывали и бросались
Врастинычну, оставить меня на земле. И свет наконец
Стал оглушительный, а всё вокруг просто белым.
И я уже больше ничего не мог различить, всё
Было одного цвета, всё было из одного света, и я
Заплакал, потому что больше не мог кричать.
И потому что вокруг стояла такая тишина. И в этот
Момент Тихий бог заговорил со мной, он сказал,
Чтобы я не пытался вскочить и броситься в сторону,
Он сказал: «Слолни», и я почувствовал, что свет
Лёг мне на лоб как рука. И я вспомнил себя в животе
У мамы и свернулся так же и лежал, пока свет шёл
Сквозь меня, словно колонны огромного небесного храма.
А потом всё кончилось, а я всё ещё лежал и смотрел,
Как свет отступает, уходит, мелкало и печально. Нет, я
Не пытался его удержать или догнать, но мне было
Так грустно, как бывает, когда смотришь – ты выиграл
В лотерею 25 тысяч, а потом поглядишь внимательней,
А это билет из прошлого розыгрыша, в общем – мимо.
И ты стоишь с ним в руке и думаешь: «Почему?»
Вот и я стоял и думал так: «Почему?» Через час примерно
Пашли меня опять мои спутники и без особых разговоров
Мы опять сели в машину и поехали. Потом вернулись в город.
И тогда я встал, умылся и пошел на работу. Теперь
В получку я жду, но ничего особенного не происходило.
Проснувшись утром, был понедельник, я лежал, утомившись лицом
В всех ранее по домам, приехали к себе и лёг спать.
Каждые выходные я езжу по этой дороге взад и вперёд,
Но не вижу на этих облаках, ни этого света. Я не могу сказать,
Что стал примерным христианином или кем-то ещё.
Да и некогда там особенно думать, работа по горло.
Лето, самый сезон. Но когда меня приласкал на радио,
Дай, думаю, пойду. Может и не один такой, может
Отыщется такой человек, по которому тоже
Похожий свет. И то было бы легче. Хотя не знаю,
О чём бы мы стали с ним говорить, так, может быть,
Помолчали бы вместе, показали бы друг другу руки
И разошлись. Но если с кем-то
Такое случится, не бойтесь, а потом – напишите мне.
Пожалуйста. Адрес в редакции. До связи!

HER OIL

Oil comes out of her kneecaps.
Her knees are oozing with oil.
On a good day you can accumulate
A half-litre bottle,
By dragging the lip along her skin,
Catching unctuous drops.
And what can you do about that?
The doctors just hold consultations;
At least they haven't sounded off to the press.
Her relatives are already used to her
Always wearing those snug black
Leggings with special padding
On the knees to soak up all the droplets.
Oil is her daily routine.
She even keeps an eye on prices,
Market fluctuations, like someone's pulse,
Slightly feverish, dynamic, alive,
And unfathomable. Lately
She feels like she's a whole
Oil-producing nation herself–
A state, confident of its own significance.
Look how she crosses the street,
How she laughs, goes shopping.
So what if she gets rid of the oil
In the bath, wiping away heavy black drops
Again and again. In this life of ours
She has oil. What have you got?

THE SYSTEM IN THE SYSTEM

He worked in the FBI strike force for ten years,
then placed a letter of resignation on
his superior's desk. He couldn't articulate
a single logical reason for this step. The personnel
division, on consideration, decided
to send him for a confidential psychological
evaluation. He sat through a string of interviews with
in-house psychologists, leading to the following
conclusions. What follows is a decoded transcript of
the February 15 interview. He says: "… After a strike
we usually searched the premises for weapons,
narcotics and other evidence. Looking in every crack.
And I began to notice: every time
I opened a refrigerator, on the top shelf there was
a peach yoghurt with an open lid,
half eaten. Next to it there were always
two overripe bananas. This came to my attention
in 2010, while capturing a suspect in Washington,
in the same year it happened again in Denver, then
in Kansas City, and then it really took off. Ultimately,
I discovered fifteen refrigerators across the entire country
with precisely this combination of items on the top
shelf. But the final straw was that last time
in New York: the apartment had a huge, white
refrigerator. On the top shelf, once again, a half-empty
container of peach yoghurt. But next to it were three (!)
overripe bananas. I thought – what the hell!
That is, I thought the same thing earlier. But this was too much.
Even in the system there's no system, get it?
No system in the system…" The verdict
of the division chief: "Congratulate the subject
with advancement to the next level. Grant him
clearance for ND; transfer him under the authority of division
for prevention of impossibilities with increase in
salary and enhanced benefits. Return to fulfilment of assigned duties."

Translated by Kevin M. F. Platt & Karina Sotnik

VIDEO: PHYSICIST

СИСТЕМА В СИСТЕМЕ

Он работал в ФБР в группе захвата, десять лет, прежде чем положил рапорт об отставке на стол начальника. Никаких логических причин для подобного шага он не мог привести. Отдел контроля личного состава, изучив вопрос, решил отправить его на закрытое психологическое освидетельствование. Он прошел через беседу с местными психологами, и вот что выяснилось обычно обыскивали квартиры на предмет оружия, от 15 февраля. Он говорит: «После заявки мы Далее следует расшифрованная запись беседы с местными психологами, и вот что выяснилось наркотиков и улик. Заглядывали во все углы. И вот что я стал замечать – каждый раз когда переснимал посуду и уже припрятанный румянец, напоминающий опустошенный, а рядом лежали два переверстах банках. Я обратил на это внимание в 2010-м, когда мы брали одного типа в Вашингтоне, и том же году это повторилось в Денвере, потом в Канзас-сити, и пошло-поехало. В конечном счете я обнаружил 15 холодильников по всей стране именно с таким набором предметов на верхней полке. Но что мне доходило – это последний случай в Нью-Йорке в квартире была огромный белый холодильник. На верхней полке снова была пустая упаковка пересохового йогурта. Но рядом лежали три переверстах банках. Я поднимал – что за ерунда! То я и раньше так думал, но это меня добило. И в системе – никаких системы, понимаете? И в системе – никаких системы...» Результаты начальника отдела: «Подправить опрошенного с переходом на новый уровень. Присвоить ему доступ NT, перевести под контроль службы предотвращения несогласного с повышенным оклада и страховых выплат. Вернуть к исполнению служебных обязанностей».

41 / 114

BUGS, BOUGHS

"I've become a bad person –
everywhere I see bad things,"
said a passenger
in an intercity bus to me
in the course of a hushed evening conversation.
"In the trees I see bugs;
in poetry – tautology;
in politicians' speeches – politicians' speeches.
Maybe it won't last forever,
and some day I'll again see
in the trees – elegance of boughs;
in poetry – generosity of nuance;
in politicians' speeches – alternatives for the future.
But for now it's like a wall. You understand,
it's just my problem. The world
is still absolutely, absolutely
magnificent." And he fell silent, looking out the window
at a house, slipping away into the dark,
with a pair of lit windows,
where they were watching a TV show, it seems,
with chocolates and strong tea.

Translated by Kevin M. F. Platt & Karina Sotnik

FORECAST

It's been ten years since I told you
That it's forever: these trees, these fields, these misfortunes,
These modest, timid successes,
These roadside cafés, peddling vacant air
And unfashionable music,
These days, when parents bring their kids
To school for the first time,
Feeling a wrenching mix of anxiety and joy;
These apples, this morning fog in the gullies,
These canned peas, glory
Of the national salad.
And you spoke of shopping malls from here to the horizon,
Stacks of glossy magazines right by the door,
Endless six-lane highways,
Driving right into the sea,
Nights that pass into days
Like one hard currency into another.
And where is all that? I ask you
At a bus stop,
Decorated with a simple announcement
Of the loss of two Dachshunds, female, with dark coloration.
It was generated on a printer
Two days ago.

BAREFOOT

I remember that girl,
We worked together in an ad agency
With grey wall-to-wall carpet on the floors,
And that hot summer she would wander across it barefoot
Giving us various assignments:
Either advertising for baby formula, or
For the European Union, or for a car brand, with a name
That in our language sounded almost exactly like "cunt."
There was even a shower there,
That the lay-out guys would use
When they showed up to work with a hangover.
And this office was located on a street,
With a name (another problematic case)
That in a neighbouring country's language could be taken for "ass."
And you would frequently run into tourists there
From that country, grinning in glee and taking selfies
Against the background of street signs posted at the corners.
That was a pure, naïve joy they had.
And that's the way it was. Summer, a sunny morning
Packs of tourists, smiling broadly
Into the lenses of disposable cameras on the corner nearby.
It was a fine place, in general,
Low key, despite the line of work,
And, probably for just that reason, even though
Our agency changed its name three times
(Each name more mysterious and
    obscure than the last),
It went up in smoke all the same.
But I remember that girl, how she
Would walk over the grey carpeting
    among the monitors,
Tables piled high with papers and coffee
    cups,
In her flower-print dress.
It just took your breath away.
Barefoot.

POPULAR SONG FOR UKULELE

Write me a novel
That will tell of another novel
All the same I'll read neither one nor the other –
I'll depart for Manchuria and perish for nothing.

Paint me a painting, one that will
Depict another painting.
All the same I'll see neither one nor the other –
I'll depart for Manchuria and perish for nothing.

Compose a song for me, with words
About a different song entirely,
All the same I'll hear neither one nor the other –
I'll depart for Manchuria and perish for nothing.

PERFORMANCE: JOE DASSIN

SOMETHING LIKE A REPORT

The cat, a nocturnal animal,
Runs around the house and talks in Spanish
Wipes the table at every opportunity,
In general, resembles a snow plough,
Left unattended with engine running.
She was here last year, too, I heard her,
How she stepped around objects, did circles under
The sofas, sweeping tracks away with her tail. And now
She's here, and you can read a mute question in her eyes:
"What was the name of the Turkish all-star football team captain
In 1951?" I could turn on the computer
And find the answer. But a whole chain of question marks
Would follow. And that would start looking more like
An interrogation. So I buy myself off with dry food
And a little bowl of water. Pretend to be her owner.
She falls asleep at dawn, having travelled a thousand roads,
Visited a thousand places, begged and received absolution.

THE RITZ

Inlaid with a blue mosaic showing
The lode stars, the floor
Of the spa-bath and the circumspect illumination
Along with the sound of running water,
As though in eternal pursuit of itself,
Puts you in a philosophical mood. Now it's
Midday and no one is around, except somewhere
In the depths behind the glass a shadow flits by
Of a dark-haired woman in white, checking
Whether there are still enough snow-white towels
And bath robes. There are more than enough. The tall
Shelves, reaching to the ceiling, are piled with rolled-up
Waffle-textured bundles. All the same, they
Don't lie close together, each has space around it,
And, just as surely, the guests here are one-offs.
After rising out of the jacuzzi and wiping yourself dry,
You put on a robe, tie the belt,
Stick your feet in white, terry-towel slippers,
And walk past the leather chaise-longues and
The sports facility, past the glass
Shelves with various body products, to come out
By the mirrors near the elevators. The doors open,
You insert your card and press the button
For your floor. You are on the eighth. 808. As though
Caught between two infinitudes. You are a lost
Participant from the conference on partnership. Due to a computer
    glitch
It's been three weeks and they haven't checked you out yet. You go to
The breakfast, where you have your own table, and leave

Chocolates in the room for the maids, young fair-haired
Girls, hopelessly polite and pedantic. The abundant
Breakfast is enough to last you all day, and in the evening you can
    grab
A kebab, and then chase rabbits on the lawns of the huge
Park. By this hour it's being criss-crossed almost exclusively
By cyclists. You sleep well, with closed windows and
The AC turned on. When they at last discover
Their mistake, you'll probably be able to hide and lie low in the depths.
So long as there is that blue mosaic.

INSTALLATION: TIME ROOM

ОТЕЛЬ РИТЦ

Выложенный голубой мозаикой
С путевыми звездами пол
Вместе с шумом струящейся воды,
SPA-бассейна и продуманная подсветка
Как будто очень затуманивают саму себя.
Настраивают на философский тон. Сейчас
Полдень и здесь никого нет, только где-то
В глубине за стеклами мелькает тело
Черноволосой женщины в белом, проверяющей
По-прежнему ли достаточно кристально чистых полотенец
И банных халатов. Их – более чем. Высокие
Полки до потолка выложены свернутыми
Вафельными рулонами. В то же время они
Лежат не вплотную, вокруг каждого есть пространство,
Ведь и посетители здесь – штучный товар.
Вдруг наешься из джакузи и наскуро интерьершь,
Ты накинешь халат, застегнувшись его,
Вставишь ноги в более махровые тапочки,
И пройдешь мимо кожанных лежанок и
Зала для занятия спортом, мимо стеклянных
Полок с разной ерундой для тела и выходишь
К зеркалам в лифту, раскрываются двери,
Ты вставляешь свою карточку и нажимаешь кнопку
Этажа. Ты живешь на восьмом, 808. Как будто
Защемленный между двумя бесконечностями. Ты – потерянный
Участник конференции по сотрудничеству. Компьютер для себя
И тебя не вычисляют уже третью неделю. Посещаешь
Завтраки, где есть свои столики, и оставляешь
В номере конфетки уборщицам, молодым светловолосым
Девушкам, отлично вежливым и педантичным. Обильного
Завтрака хватает на целый день, а вечером можно перехватить
Кебаб, а потом пойти потолочь зайцев на лужайках огромного
Парка. В это время его пересекают почти исключительно
Велосипедисты. Спишь ты хорошо, с закрытыми окнами и
Ошибусь, то скорее всего тебе удастся скрыться и лечь на дно.
Лишь бы там была голубая мозайка.

POSTCOMMUNICATION

Contact us;
pay for services;
accept our congratulations;
place your faith in us.
Print this out at your leisure,
recalculate your rate,
distribute current
in the network,
surround the roundness.
And one more thing.
At the present moment
all operators are busy.
Does this mean that at the next –
they'll be free and happy?
prosperous and successful?
Independent and tranquil?

FIGURES OF SPEECH

The touching, naive, somehow sincere
Fighter jet flew over the river. The ripe,
Pomaded tank cosily set its treads down,
Approaching the woods. Intimately, childishly, a thump
Was heard from the salvo fire system. Happy, contented
Infantrymen ran off somewhere. Growing in the sky were
Smoky, blooming flowers of explosions.
A slight, stubby general promised
To seize everything possible by midnight. The happy
Mischievous correspondent held before him
A microphone with the number of his channel. TV-viewers
Rejoiced and puffed up in bliss at the broadcast.
The soapy war foamed up before them in all
Its unctuous lustre. The sun shimmered.

Трогательный, наивный, какой-то искренний
Истребитель пролетел над речкой. Спелый
Напомаженный танк уютно перебирал гусеницами,
Подъезжая к лесу. Заветно, по-детски бабахнула
Установка залпового огня. Счастливые довольные
Пехотинцы куда-то побежали. В небе росли
Дымчатые раскрывавшиеся цветки взрывов.
Небольшой коренастый генерал обещал
Взять всё, что можно, до полуночи. Весёлый
Озорной корреспондент держал перед ним
Микрофон с номером канала. Телезрители
Радовались и блаженно отдувались от трансляции.
Мыльная война пенилась перед ними во всём
Своём маслянистом блеске. Сверкало солнце.

ФИГУРЫ РЕЧИ

QUESTIONS

Have we held enough blackberry in the palms of our hands,
Or cloudberry, cranberry? Didn't suspiciously many
Unripe berries come our way, or to the contrary,
Slightly bruised ones, a little brown on the sides?
Have we stepped softly over carpets of August woods?
Flicked flashlights on at night's darkest hour?
Worked in sawmills – as mysterious, taciturn
Figures, wiping away the sweat? Slept on hillocks
Arms thrown wide? Gradually become the model of
Messy, incomprehensible handwriting? Left
Palm prints in the sandy banks of an unhurried
Stream? Untangled obdurate, taut branches?
Have we lived our lives well to the present moment?
Always been in the right? Did we miss something important?

PERFORMANCE: HER OIL

ВОПРОСЫ

"Достаточно ли мы держали в ладонях ежевики,
морошки, клюквы? Не подозрительно ли много
попадалось нам незрелых ягод или, наоборот,
уже слегка подавленных, с коричневыми боками?
Ступали ли мы мягко по коврам августовских лесов?
Зажигали ли фонарики в самое темное время суток?
Работали ли на лесопилках молчаливыми загадочными
фигурами, утиравшими пот? Спали ли на пригорках,
разметав руки? Становились ли постепенно примерами
неразборчивого неаккуратного почерка? Оставляли
ли отпечатки ладоней в прибрежном песке у неспешной
речки? Распутывали ли не поддающиеся тугие ветки?
Хорошо ли мы прожили жизнь до сегодняшнего момента?
Всегда ли мы были правы? Не пропустили ли что-то важное?

FIELD TRIPS

All the sad jeans of the seventies
(not to be confused with the happy jeans of the sixties,
or the rowdy jeans of the fifties)
were tied up in a single bundle
and confined in an abandoned quarry
somewhere near Pittsburgh.
Once in a while they even bring in field-trips
from nearby schools.
"Why are the jeans sad?" ask the children.
"We don't know," answer the teachers.
"We can only guess," say the teachers.
"We can't really remember," admit the teachers.

VLADIMIR SVETLOV

* * *

on avenu avenue
after the end of the world
above the accidental survivors
in the concrete cell
they lay on the floor
in the window embrasure
a cold wind
drove snowflakes
but the cold
is no barrier
to addressees lacking bodies
the cold as easy as pie
we're warmed up
by sparks of contact
of electricity
our lives superseded
by a signal
an accumulated charge
the string yes-yes-no
flash
glimmer
silence

RADIO: MARX FM

на авеню авеню
после конца света
над случайно спасшимися
в бетонной клетке
лежали на полу
в проёмину окна
холодный ветер
задувал снежинки
но холод
не преграда
лишённым тела адресатам
холод ничуём
нас согревают
искр касания
электричества
нам заменяет жизнь
сообщение
сигнал
накопленный заряд
цепочка да-да-нет
отблеск
мерцание
тишина

* * *

from this our tenderness
everything bursts at the seams and spills out
the tailor obligingly at the ready
holds silk and scissors
now you sew, now cut yourself
fingers all pricked
you rush around, curse, get huffy
lie-truth-cut
and prick yourself again
wink conspiratorially
smile at who knows who
after a long disturbed sleep
can't get rested can't wake up

INSTALLATION: THE CORNER HOUSE [KGB HQ]

от этой нашей нежности
все трещит по швам и сыплется
портной наготове услужливо
держит шелк и ножницы
то зашиваешь, то режешься
пальцы все исколоты
и снова колешься
мечешься, материшься, хорохоришься
врешь-правду-режешь
неизвестно кому улыбаешься
заговорщически подмигиваешь
после долгого сна тревожного
не выспишься, не напросыпаешься

* * *

what'll you say?

what will you say
when the day comes
party and night will end
fun and happiness
will end
everything will end
wholly
what will you say?

just as he thought
that there's too much love
too much
too much love
too much
memories
detaining for a night
no more
no longer

room's a mess

в комнате не убрано
на дворне
на больше
которые удержать на ночь
воспоминания
слишком
слишком много любви
слишком
что слишком много любви
как он думал

что ты скажешь?
целиком
все закончится
закончится
развлечения и радость
вечеринка и ночь закончатся
когда придет день
что ты скажешь

что скажешь?

***

let's depart for where they caught us
we'll finish where they found us
in a rewind of
the touch of hands and lips
we'll steal that kiss and forget
taste of lips, hand movements, back's arch
don't remember your name at all
we'll start dressing one another
more tenderly than anyone has ever dressed
buckles, buttons, all in place?
suddenly in the elevator the scent vanishes
almost got to taxi, but first the tip
it's all the same to the waitress
crappy coffee, after that I don't remember…
who is that girl?!?!?!?

давай уйдём туда, где нас застали
закончим там, где нас нашли
в обратной перемотке
прикосновений рук и губ
снимаем поцелуй и забываем
вкус губ, движение рук, изгиб спины
совсем не помню, как тебя зовут
мы станем одевать друг друга
так нежно, как никто не одевал
застежки, пуговицы, всё ли на месте?
вдруг в лифте исчезает запах
не успели до такси, сначала чаевые
официанту наплевать и так
кофе дерьмовый, дальше не помню…
кто эта девушка?!?!?!?

THE BEAUTIFUL

people flounder at skin's edge
where light ends
the scent of artificial fur
is sensed
if
one follows a half-step behind
it is brought by air
a movement
which arises simply
because two people are walking
so
one may
turn attention to those
who consider the beautiful to be the similar
they wear identical soles
and pick out lip colour for others
but one may
seek out others
yet even they
are dissimilar
similar to others just as dissimilar
and so beauty becomes
a matter of random choice

* * *

say "raisin," baby
and it'll get sweet
the tip of your tongue –
show it to me just a bit
your body calls, your body beckons
your body weeps
you little candy baby
you lollipop of cool sweetness
in the corners of your lips
the meaning of your embraces is simple,
love me, baby, love
and with pathos, in low tones
sung from the stomach
my life – a tangle
unwind its threads
and roll it up
not to be found again

PERFORMANCE @ NICE PLACE, RIGA

CONFIDENTIAL CONVERSATION

i don't know why he began that conversation
and called it confidential
i picked him up on the highway
the car radio was being torn apart
by hysterical synthesizers and guitars from the eighties
he began mysteriously poetically about kisses in the shadow of
    doubts
as though he were spying on me
and concealing his discoveries in notebooks
he was spying on me, but wanted to confess
changed his expression, didn't come near
and he was in a strange t-shirt
extremely washed out
the best girls
are dead girls
was written on it
they never
say no
and then he started off again, about
golden flecks on the black water
he says gotta
get beneath them
and look from inside
at
golden flecks on the black water

i never saw him again after that
as he got out he screamed he'd throw a rock
through my windscreen
don't believe me?
he screamed
i was calm
don't know why

CLICK, CLICK

click, click
I shoot emaciated models for a tome
click, click
I dance with the minister of regional development
for a cover
click, click
I shoot a young guy
for the sex services pages header
click, click
he likes small animals
and wants to become a vet
for this big zoo
rural guys
like large animals
cows, pigs, horses
but he likes small ones
so if our little dog gets sick
I know who to go to.
click, click
recently saw some wild horses
what a strange sight!
click, click
they're the most pointless creatures
I don't mean the ones that graze in the
    distance
and run off faster than the wind
if you come up close
they're not averse to the human caress
also sexual in nature,
all day they chomp away in one place,
and cavort with the foals
but if a star shows up on the forehead
from crossbred ancestors
then they might not accept a given horse
into the herd
click, click
there's also a wild cow in that preserve
but it wandered off somewhere
click, click

HIT PARADE

like a gift for loyalty
to repeat customers
we have been given these days
days of happiness
of smiles and understanding glances
days of angels signing resonantly with horns
with eyes slightly feral from derision
there's reason enough to despise us
and also to slice our throats
there's plenty we can be accused of
but angels in their armour of diamonds
shine even on cloudy days
their songs never fall silent…
now that's what i'd really like to do
to spend the rest of my days
composing a hit-parade
of the 100 best songs
of all times and nations

INSTALLATION: TWINKLING CRYSTAL

MONEY

hapless middleman
in the eternal race
no way to resist
the flow of beauty towards money –
it'll wash you away
you hang on
in futility
say money
is no problem
if there's money
and every time
you freeze in place
groping, like for a pulse
at your wallet
severely
diminished in thickness
so that with cold hands
you can exchange your last coins
for one more wish
and if my girl
were money
you'd like her more

ДЕНЬГИ

посредник неудачный
в вечной гонке
потока красоты к деньгам
тебе не устоять –
снесет
напрасно
цепляешься
говоришь что деньги
не проблема
если деньги есть
и каждый раз
ты будешь замирать
нащупывать как пульс
бумажник
изрядно
потерявший в толщине
чтобы холодными руками
на последние монеты
еще одно желание променять
и если б девушка моя
была деньгами
любил бы больше

EMPTY AIRPORT

empty airport
planes
sleeping
a pastor picks up white doves at customs
the holy spirit here for a show in the park
excited poodles hobnob on the way to the taxi
a circus show
to catch trusting souls
you take some instant photos
the bar is closed at night
the church is open
in the airport
concrete and wood
can't recall the architect
a prize last year
we drive on
to the sea
trees still have leaves
lit by street lamps from below
with black light reflected from the asphalt
sea thick like oil
becomes motionless before us
flirtations of man with sea are so naive
all these fishing boats
and bathing at the shore in summer
what is it?
in this black
mass that repulses us
a desire to get as far away as possible
quickly
we walk through nighttime jūrmala
in hopes that in at least one café
the bartender is awake
but in vain

*Translated by Kevin M. F. Platt &
Natalia Fedorova*

CLASSMATE

it was good times,
but communications were complicated
instead of facebook people carried around packs of photos
of personal moments
walkman playing in the ears,
they would pass it around to listen
if they liked something
would ask to make a recording
now
we discuss
whether those waiters were sincere
when they smiled
or are they forced to do that?
and they're making this huge effort to smile?
and take those
young
beautiful people
who spend more on their image than on life
wandering forever through swamp mud
to get a single shot by the river in a clean suit

back then movies and the stars were the real thing
if they twinkled, no one knew
except their friends and family

gays still wanted to get adopted
by Madonna, and then by Tori Amos
alternately

and that's how the story ended

without kids in first grade
with adopted parents
it seems like now the Parisians remember
how Benjamin Clementine sang in the metro and on the street
and by the way where is that guy now,
remember?
who swam through rivers,
crossed borders
to get to Paris on foot,
before they could deport him again?
the squares are closed at night,

now it's clear why,
and it seems it'll be like that here soon, too,
he says

and he also says
one girl told all about
the horror of life in a family with multiple kids
can't find your things in the morning
someone's already mistaken them for their own.

have you noticed we use the word "to tell" about posts in FB?

INSTALLATION: RADIO WALL

ARTŪRS PUNTE

* * *

The path to his stone on the high dune
leads through an airy forest of pine,
tall, straight, with sunlight glancing through the crowns
as though celebrating the retreat of the sea millennia ago
but "we pass through as though feeling our way
at night in the hallways of an apartment
with glue-gun in hand, afraid of stepping
on an abandoned toy,
something like a vacuum-cleaner filter"
that's what this reminds me of, you announce
and I've got nothing to say
for a while we stand quietly by the stone with the photograph
until you find the right words once more
"And you know there was this time he and I were kissing
after a concert." What can you say after that?
"I can give you a lift back"
Drive the car in drawn-out silence, that's all I'm good at.

VIDEO: TALLINAS STREET

MNEMONICS

It's a good thing all the same that I took a course to improve memory that time.

Needed to remember her birthday, and just made a sentence in which the number of letters in each word corresponded to the successive numbers in the date, and was golden.

Then wanted to wish her happy birthday in French, and for phonetic recall used Russian words of unrelated meaning that sounded similar, just like they taught.

In order to remember better the book she gave as a gift, made notes in the margins while reading, and it really did help, even though I never looked back at them later on.

From the names of perfumes and fashion designers that she mentioned most frequently I made up a little song (it's a mnemonic device), that I could sing to myself when looking for a present for her.

After we started living together I never wrote down a shopping list, memorizing it instead using the method of an exciting story in which the things we needed played key roles.

Or even now when I wanted to remember forever that trip we took to Liepaja, I just collected everything in intense visual images and set them out on bookshelves in my mind, like photographs.

I took all the plans that we made for the future but never actually realized and made a rhyming list, resulting in a funny little poem – now there's no way I'll ever forget that.

And in order not to forget by the morning the phrase that will absolutely bring her back and that won't let me sleep at the moment, there's a simple solution: keep a notepad and pen by the bedside.

In general, I started to keep a diary, something like reminiscences, so that our time together won't fade away from unreliable memory; maybe something like a book or a long poem will come of it.

There's also a plan to immortalize her memory for real – to collect signatures to rename a street; of course, everyone will think it's in honour of her historical namesake, but I'll know the truth.

It'd be even better to put up a monument in the centre, on the banks of the canal, and then she'd remain in memory forever; though unfortunately there's no physical resemblance between them…

But when it comes to her hair, when it unexpectedly bared her shoulders, or the moon appearing from behind her hips, her breast's weight in the hand, the warmth of our bed at weekends, the taste of long kisses on a sleepless night, the scent of embracing at the needlessness of words, the voice that resounded suddenly after a long silence, and all the other awful memories like that – I have no idea how to forget it all.

HIGHWAY

If you live in a village
considered by most who drive through
just an annoying reason
to put on the brakes
and those who do pass by each day
exceed in number
the local population by several times over
then it should be immediately clear to you
how suspicious it is to see
a private car in the shadows
parked in front of a truck
on the narrow shoulder of the tunnel
cut by the freight traffic
through the crowns of the trees…
what's that under the canvas sheeting
what's behind the smoked windows
at the back…
maybe nothing at all
just a coincidence

VIDEO: SO THAT IS HOW

* * *

Through the rustle of the earth works
it takes a long while to reach our field
before appearing on the incline of the highway
coming from the Estonian border
at first as a speeding point
a black rider clinging
in sculptural clothing and
threateningly pulling
with a dark motorcycle
empty Sunday air
deep into our locale until
by the lines of the body, wrapped
around the motorcycle and long, thin
hair from under the helmet
we recognize fragile pale Liina
responsible in the Tallinn library
for book digitization
then the scene comes into focus
pierced at the point of refusal
by her disappearance
and in the re-established quiet
in pursuit of that metal, pulled from the earth
we sense that our alert thought
cannot even begin to give chase
no, Liina, we ourselves believe only in
what we can touch with our hands.

ONE-AND-A-HALFTH FLOOR

The ceiling slopes
so you can only stand up
in the middle
but there's room for everyone to lie down
all the same it's better than in a tent
the roof overhead
got so hot in the day
you can't even breathe
and can't open windows
boarded up
for last winter
even so mosquitos managed to get in
can't understand but anyhow
for some reason you decide on this option

TRIP TO THE CITY

In the reply from the number chosen at random
you get the address of one of those houses in the centre
with glass cupolas over the entrance halls that
let in daylight for illumination of the stairwells
and at night shine light back out above the roofs

The code entered with an error all the same opens
the stranger's apartment, though it's already full of your stuff
where unknown people all smelling of the same shower gel
embrace you, calling you by arbitrary names
after just one correct gesture all desire disappears

Forgetting about the paint on your fingers you touch your face
and in the mirror see how well the moss covers
your neat silvery beard
so that the single desire that is now possible
is to stay like this as long as possible – for many more years

INSTALLATION: OBJECT NO. 3

* * *

Today I understood
that I have never yet in my life
typed the word anklebone
and I've never had occasion
to write it longhand either
as far as I can recall
how could that be
anklebone anklebone anklebone
are there many other words like that
how can one know
are you typing out every character to me
or just copying your
goodbye goodbye goodbye goodbye
goodbye goodbye goodbye goodbye

WRONG SEASON

The volume displaced in the overall landscape
by the building of the village church, is equal to
the day that we gave away to acquaintances
that child's seat we didn't need any longer
the day I grasped that the sounds of the desiccated organ
no longer elevate my spirit
Although in the scrub forest
in the peat bog I can inertly
observe for a long while
how boots slowly displace the land

PUBLICATION: CONTEMPORARY RUSSIAN POETRY

НЕ СЕЗОН

Объем, вытесненный в общем пейзаже
зданием сельской церкви, равен
тому дню, когда мы за ненадобностью
отдали знакомым детское сдвижное
дно, когда в пойме, что звуки рассохшегося органа
больше не возносят мой дух
зато среди низкорослого леса
на торфяных топях, могу долго
отрешенно наблюдать,
как сапоги понемногу теснят дно.

NOW HIRING

A programmer-developer
Accountant-record keeper
Project manager
Certified land surveyor
Mechanic for freight trucks
Shower installer
Salesman-consultant
Translator from Swedish...
All are wanted
Even a specialist in acoustic physics
Can at times find
Appropriate employment here...
Without help, even the weight of a body
At the moment of impact with the ground
After falling from my balcony
I wouldn't be able to calculate
And I can't say that I've read a lot
And remember practically nothing of that...
No, I also don't know Anders Petersen
Oh, right, I guess I've seen the works
But didn't remember the name

* * *

She prepared well:
broke up with her boyfriend
quit her job
rented out the apartment she bought with loans
sold her car
gave her girlfriends all her stuff
and her discount cards
transferred all her music to mp3s
deleted her profile and her old mail
bought a new laptop
visited her grandmother and aunts
taught her mother how to text
made peace with her younger sister
stopped eating meat, reading the news
finally retuned her sheet music to the library
signed up for some useful LISTSERVS.
Waved down a truck with her "Berlin" sign
and didn't say a single word through all of Poland…
And now, several rented apartments later
falling asleep alone in a room with walls
painted white by the previous tenants
she peers into the dark air, where
someone's invisible presence can be clearly felt
she listens to herself – if only she could know for sure
that now this is really it,
now everything is how it should be.

Translated by Kevin M. F Platt & Michael Wachtel

* * *

to S.T.

Peculiar things are at times fastened
to window frames on façades of buildings,
alright, a birdfeeder, or a rearview mirror,
two even, a basket or, imagine,
a rusty little bell – on a fourth-floor window.
I believe there's an explanation for everything
and so, literally by a few gestures, I managed to establish
that our pal here came to us from Pärnu,
whereas that girl, for example, emerged whole from a newspaper
and from now on will sit behind a cash register,
and all just because it has fewer keys…
Is it worth pretending to be a simple passer-by any longer?
How long can you squint at rooftops,
and flinch at stray droplets?
Who needs the little bell and for what purpose
(variation: the rearview mirror) on a fourth-floor window?
What are people from your past doing here?
Their slight smiles are at whose expense?
Who will make sure in your absence
that jars in the kitchen are full: tea, coffee, sugar?
What else? In your explanatory note
give short answers in simple form.

* * *

to VL

Where were you led by the keyword search
for your own name, following the links,
you suddenly find yourself twenty years later
in an apartment without a single book,
without bookshelves.
Your town has completely gone to seed, and never
(you can watch the weather forecast to the end)
never on a single channel
will the meteorologist mention it.
(Weather takes shape at random.)
Yet the heating is set old-man high, which ruins teeth,
and cooking like old ladies, like unwashed carrot runts
(you work a market stall until dark) sleepily
your fingers part – the remote falls
the remote falls and the remote fell to the floor… Caught a cold,
you get tangled up in plain sheets, oversleep, are roused
(tormented by bills, a neighbour rages through every wall),
you throw a questioning glance at wallpaper, in this shot
you've not yet been subjected to the iron of domesticity,
your marriage is still supported by overwhelming credit,
the house is still mortgaged, and still – the computer
is more sensitive to spikes in the current than you
to shifts in pressure, and suddenly you come to your senses;
on the last day of the week they shut down the network;
you take a stroll, try to shut
all active window, ask for books,
at the least the ones for poor folk: one
    hundred ways to get rich,
to repair karma, answers in ten steps, …
how to get married, lose weight…
How can I get out of here?

***

Metatarsal, tarsal, phalanges of the digits
Metatarsal, tarsal, phalanges of the digits.
Put on dark glasses and repeat these words.
Beyond the lenses gleams a kind of depth,
but it can't be said aloud
beyond the words gleams a kind of depth,
but it can't be said aloud
in poets there appears a kind of depth
a kind of void a kind of void a kind of void
Metatarsal, tarsal, phalanges of the digits –
this is poetry, this is verse.

INSTALLATION: SIGNALLING PAIRS

A YEAR'S TIME

August
all I can do this evening
is pull in next to your building and park
this dusty van of mine with the words
tropical fruits on the side
and promise that before work in the morning
we'll definitely drive out to the beach
while the weather's this nice
but all the same it'll turn out we oversleep…
they say the outskirts will burn up along with summer

October
and then the tree in our yard – the chestnut –
will get pruned by the tenth month's singed edge
into the shape of the city tower,
as you can tell by a sure sign:
see, for days its leaves have been
turned inside out
it's harder for a tree to do that

January
than it is to signal helplessness to a hostage
in a country where no one
ever comes to their aid
in order not to set precedents
you understand charred stumps
charred stumps
out the window all winter

April
that's what there'll be…
but for the time being the day illuminates
two sides of every building
I'll reveal the secret of my
    sadness to you:
this spring I made a
    plaster mask
from a living friend's face
for which I'm being
    punished it seems

* * *

It happened that a girl from Dzhokhar Dudaev Street took a
    liking to me
I avoided her worked a lot and was always saying I was busy

later I took a closer look at the girl from Dzhokhar Dudaev Street
we became close and I worked a lot inspired by our love

but it wasn't meant to last and I dumped the girl from Dzhokhar
    Dudaev Street
and began working a lot so she wouldn't get on my nerves with
    her love

no I think it's no good I've got to get that girl from Dzhokhar
    Dudaev Street back
but she'd already found someone else and I had to work a lot to
    try to forget her

now apparently they're going to rename the street and then
    probably
everything will settle in place and I'll be able to take care of
    business in peace.

VIDEO: GUEST WORKERS

ORBITA AT THEWATERFRONT, HULL, 2017

PHOTOS: TONY WARD

СЕМЁН ХАНИН

* * *

нарисуется на автовокзале
анекдот с вот такой бородой
вот с такой прикушенной лопатой
жили-были чукча, эстонец и старый еврей
немец, француз и русский в одном лице
встретились сердце, печень и селезенка
остался без денег а сам из межгорода
отстал от автобуса негде остаться
на билет не хватает ровно вот столько
но если можете больше то конечно
она говорит съезди встреть родных
ну и поехал а их уже несколько дней
как не стребовать врожденный должок
в зале пустых ожиданий ночуешь за ауро
поезда шумят не поспишь особо
канал подмывает опоры снизу
в стекляшке над диспетчерской посидишь
сразу на сто грамм река видней
слышней кто едет вдруг объявят родных
слетаются чайки с базарных ангаров
чуют бутерброд в глубине буфета
найден бумажник потерявшего просят
проследовать к стойке информации
хватается за сердце, за портмоне
за автопортрет потертый на документ
паспорт намертво с карточкой слипся
потерян кошелек нашедшего просят
тает очередь в шестую кассу
на остановке трамвая опять толпа
где кастрюля? впустую горит табло
громкоговоритель за живое прямо
  берет
на восьмой платформе начинается
  посадка
полезай в грузовой отсек к чемоданам
отправляйся в свой межгород родной
встретиться с той что тебя послала
песня ее из колодца льется

at the bus station takes shape
a story a really old saw
a got-no-hack-eyed tale
once upon a time a Chukchi, an Estonian, and an Old Jew
a German, Frenchman, and Russian in one person
met, a heart, liver, and a spleen
ran out of cash and from out of town
late for the bus no place to lay head
need a bit more to buy a ticket
if you can spare any extra then of course
go meet your relations at the station, she says
so up and went but it's been days and no sight
can't not demand a little loan, all in the family
one buck to spend the night in the waiting for nothing area
noisy trains can't really sleep
the canal splashing against foundations below
sit in the glassy café above the dispatcher's booth
after a glass or two the river comes in focus better
hear departures better maybe they'll announce the relations
seagulls fly in from the market pavilions
sensing bread and sausage in the buffet's depths
pocketbook found would ow ner please
proceed to information counter
grab a heart, at billfold
at crumpled self-portrait on ID
passport's stuck fast to the card
lost wallet has anyone found it
a crowd again at the tram stop
where's the pan? line display burns bright for nothing
loudspeaker really hits hard
now boarding on platform number eight
climb into the freight compartment with the bags
head off to your native out of town
to meet with the one who sent you off
her song pouring from the well

* * *

нащупывая губами горлышко
пить записки из брошенных в море бутылок
проборматывая темноватые местами каракули
гортанно-кудрявое бульканье пузырьков

артикулируя тщательно в формулах вежливости скомканные
    начала

захлебываясь диким смехом
вникать в подробности катастрофы

корабль утонул
и солнце сморщилось
и море опрокинувшись разлилось
и мы тут
мы тут
тут

мы, ваши суррогатные братья и сестры
по разуму, конечно, по чему же еще
хоть бы заемному, хоть бы и внеземному
есть ли разница в этой стадии амнезии
вкусившим от неземного блаженства

мы, те самые, желеобразные небожители
затерянные в железобетонных
    необитаемых джунглях
стоим в три погибели как еще
    неоткрытые лжеорангутанги
на невозделанном побережье
    вожделенного шампанзее
ждем сигнала и умираем от
    жажды

тут поплыли чернила
и сквозь розовые, синеватые линзы
    медуз
мелькнули обмылки плоских
    невыразительных лиц

lips groping for the mouths
of bottles cast into the sea
groping to drink their messages
mumbling through scribbles, obscure in places,
the guttural, whorled gurgle of bubbles

painstakingly articulating in polite formulas the crumpled beginnings

choking on wild laughter
to penetrate the details of the catastrophe

the ship sank
and the sun shriveled up
and the capsized sea spilled out
and we're here
we're here
here

we, your surrogate brothers and sisters
related by reason, naturally – how else –
extraneous reason maybe, extraterrestrial maybe
does it make any difference at this degree of amnesia
for those who have tasted unearthly bliss

we, the very same gelatinous heavenly creatures
lost in the uninhabited reinforced concrete jungles
standing deathly contorted like undiscovered pseudoorangutans
on the uncultivated coast of a longed-for Champansee
we're waiting for the signal and dying of thirst

here the ink became blurred
and through pink and blue jellyfish lenses
were seen the washed-out remains of
flat impassive faces

***

вот такая история из того времени, когда я еще воровал
промышлял в пригородных районах, выставлял частные дома
как-то раз забрался к какой-то семейной паре, они уже спали
я шел через спальню, они там в огромной кровати, он –
    уставив лицо
в потолок, она – разметавшись, в ночнушке, и оба
разговаривали во сне, я на цыпочках встал у стены, он сказал:
«я не верю тебе, твои слова на два дня, потом они снова
станут картонкой, ложью…» – и свистнул носом. она помолчала,
вздохнула: «нитяные… вот здесь и вот здесь… в нашей
    ложе сидят…»
«ничего, – он как будто ответил, и глухо: – она уже тоже пришла»,
а она засмеялась, серьезно, смеялась – недолго, но часто,
    заливисто
«не трогай, – голос дрогнул, – не смей». он прихрюкнул, и я уже
собрался двинуться дальше, когда он отчетливо произнес: «стекла,
стекла вмерзли в лед, осколки, спрячь… меня спрячь, не могу…
убиваешь…», а она говорила в то же время: «нет курка, нет у нас их,
обратитесь к коллекционерам…» и на последнем слове она,
    казалось,
совершенно изнемогла. я вынес из этой истории горсть
    серебряных
украшений и портсигаров. я знал тогда, что за всеми картинами
– сейфы,
под всеми обоями – зеркала. вот так-то, мои дорогие, так-то вот, мои
уважаемые господа.

let me tell you a story from when I was still a burglar
I plied my trade in the suburbs, cleaned out private residences
one time I wound up with this married couple, they were already sleeping
I was going through the bedroom, they were in this huge bed, him facing up
towards the ceiling and her flopped out in a nightie, and both
were talking in their sleep, so I stand there on my tip toes by
the wall and he says:
"I don't believe you, your words are good for a couple of days, then they
turn into cardboard, lies…" then he wheezed through his nose. She was silent,
then sighed: "woven… right here and here… sitting in our box…"
"no matter," he seemed to reply, then hollowly "she's already here,"
and then she began to laugh, for real, in short spurts, but often and piercingly
"don't you touch me," her voice trembled, "don't dare." He snorted and I was
already getting ready to move on, when he clearly pronounced: "glass,
glass has frozen into the ice, shards, hide… hide me, I can't…
you're killing me," while she was saying at the same time: "there's no firing pin,
we don't have any, you might ask a collector…" and with the last word she seemingly
completely ran out of energy. To this episode I owe a handful of silver
jewellery and portcigars. I knew that behind every picture was a safe,
and behind all of the wallpaper were mirrors. It was just like that, dear friends,
just like that, respected gentlemen.

***

я ехал на велике, который сперли потом
с подружкой, с которой мы через год расстались
по улице, которую всю перестроили
в кафе – его просто потом закрыли

мы беспечно болтали, то языком, то ногами

на месте этого кафе теперь пиццерия
я даже захожу туда
заказываю себе пиццу с четырьмя сырами
мне приносят ее и разрезы на пицце
напоминают мне велосипедные спицы

вот так, спицы – пиццы

но сейчас, когда я ехал на велике
со своей милой подружкой
по всем известной улице
в наше любимое кафе
я ведь совсем не думал, что каждым нажимом педали
я тоже подталкивал этот мир к энтропии и хаосу

хотя пицца оказалась вполне себе ничего

I was riding my bike, the one that got stolen afterwards
with my girlfriend, the one I broke up with a year later
along that street that got completely rebuilt
to that café – later on it simply closed

we were happily rattling off our thoughts and our legs

now there's a pizzeria where the café used to be
I even go there sometimes
and order a four-cheese pizza
they bring it to me and the knife strokes through the pizza
remind me of spokes on a wheel

just like that: bike spokes – knife strokes

but just now, when I was riding on my bike
with my sweet girlfriend
along that well-known street
to our favourite café
I didn't stop to think that with every push on the pedals
I was also driving the world into entropy and chaos

although the pizza wasn't bad at all

***

как-то глупо прощаться заранее
эта вечность с небольшими перерывами
настоящими трещинами в поддельном мраморе
и едва ли кто просил говорить о нешуточных прорехах
но и в этих пределах простор для сомнений есть

стоит ли сейчас или после или совсем потом
в позе мокрого дерева у подозрительно белой глухой стены
инстинктивно озвучивать взгляд соскользнувший
    с еще непроявленных поляроидных потолков
с самодельных разбухших зеркал
не удержавшись в неровном мраморном свете

PERFORMANCE: SPAM

it's kind of dumb to say goodbye in advance
this eternity with small breaks
real fractures in fake marble
and did anyone even suggest mentioning the significant gaps
yet within these constraints space for doubt exists

is it worth it now or afterwards or much later
holding the pose damp tree by suspiciously white blank wall
to voice instinctively the glance sliding
from still undeveloped Polaroid ceilings
from home-made swollen mirrors
losing its grip in the uneven marble light

* * *

бронзоволицая статуя
рабыня с зубами слоновой кости
за два дня до аукциона
оказалась больна

изогнулась
так ломит суставы
ноют трещины в слишком тонких запястьях
от боли до крови прокусила коралловую губу

парализована страхом глядит
от напряжения затекла, онемела шея
отнялась и безвольно упала рука
смятую в кулаке уронила записку

опытный реставратор
прильнул к ней вправляя
смещённый мраморный позвонок
шепчет «не бойтесь, немного хрустнет»
стынут закипевшие было в груди слёзы

обрабатывает то место
где расплылась и подсохла клякса
на побелевших костяшках пальцев
из своих усов он делает щётку
чистит сколы, швы, подмышки, в шагу и клеймо

потом она только вздрогнет
на стук молотка
и будет невольно дичиться
когда новый хозяин поцокает языком

bronze-faced statue
slave girl with ivory teeth
two days before the auction
became ill

contorted
joints aching
fractures throb in overly thin wrists
coral lip bitten, bloodied from pain

paralysed in fear, she stares
neck deadened from strain, numb
one limp arm has fallen insensibly
note crumpled in fist, now dropped

the experienced conservator
has cosied up to her, resetting
the dislodged marble backbone
whispers "don't be afraid, it'll crack a bit"
about to boil over, tears cool

he works over the spot
where a smear has dried and hardened
on whitened knuckles
makes a brush from his whiskers
cleans up chips, seams, underarms, instep and maker's mark

later she'll tremble
at the mallet's strike
and instinctively recoil
when her new owner clicks his tongue

* * *

замурлыканный до бесчувствия, до онемения мочек
полярный оракул встанет сегодня не с той ноги
комочек шпаргалки сплюнет и шредеру скормит
шнуруя ботинок ляжет на холод бетона, приладит
рупор ко рту, репетируя про себя: «волосы отпустить»
«выторговать каникулы», «выпустить им чернила»

чернила теряют цвет от его науськиваний. сегодня
и их постоянство не вечно. рупор заткнут шпаргалкой.
объясняться придется на пальцах, будет гудеть
вместо вас вывихнутый на прошлой войне мизинец.
беспорядочно маша позолочеными ручками
вслед поездам предзнаменований на тупиковой ветке,

бросит прохожий сквозь зубы сакраментальный прощай.

и снова надавай обещаний и сам поверь им.

[The following text appears rotated 180° at the bottom of the page:]

overpurred to senselessness, to numbed earlobes
the polar oracle will get up today on the wrong side of the bed
spit out the balled up cheat-sheet and feed it to the shredder
lie on the concrete's cold to lace up a boot, position the
megaphone at his lips, repeating to himself: "let hair grow long"
"weasel out a vacation," "train their ink away"

the ink loses colour from his hounding. today
even its permanence ain't forever. the cheat-sheet will plug the megaphone
have to explain things with hand-waving, instead of your voice
the pinkie you sprained in the last war will be ringing.
erratically waving his little gold-leafed hands
in the wake of trains of portents on a dead-end branch line,

a passer-bye, through his teeth, tosses off a sacramental goodbye.

so hand out once again promises and believe in them yourself

* * *

и боишься, и ждешь, когда он наступит
тот день, когда ты окончательно поймешь
что мир держится не на слонах и китах
а на маленьких беспокойных хомячках

и ты узнаешь, что вавилон
располагается в верманском парке
где девы лежат на картонных возвышениях
в пышных париках изображают львов

и разверстые бездны закроют двери
и у первого троллейбуса опустятся штанги
не держась руками, двинутся в обратный путь
экономки с матвеевского рынка

и выйдут резервисты на детские площадки
нетвердыми ногами по резиновой крошке
чтобы совсем отличить красные качели
от зеленой горки, от желтой лошадки

и наполнятся вазы на фасаде оперы
теплыми еще плодами юга
и прозреют бобры в своих хвостах
расплющенную ногу мариса лиепы

и воды в даугаве станут бирюзовыми
в назидание своим многочисленным притокам
и повернутся головы на французском посольстве
посмотреть как из оперной трубы валит черный дым

и альпинист сквозь тернии пробъется к вершине вантов
и отъедет последнее такси от бара чомски
и бернар тогда наденет пальто и шляпу
а лачплеша станет прямой и без горок

и пустынник заблудится в базаре берга
чемоданным колесиком стуча по плитке
и вмажут факелом этим мужланам
девушки на входе в сплендид-пэлес

и съехавшие съемщики обманутым вкладчицам
нашепчут на ухо много лишнего
как из темных каналов бьют фонтаны
как из теплых стран приезжают загорелыми

и симпатизанты сотрут с лица улыбки
приняв за вокзал очередной супермаркет
и переедет поездом ставшую реку
и вторым номером переедет еще раз

и взойдут звезды из рук свободы
и из хлябей хлынет грибной дождик
и мы ляжем с тобой на газон под гинкго
и попробуем лежать совсем неподвижно

you fear and anticipate, when will it come –
that day, when you will at last understand
that the world stands not on the backs of elephants and whales
but of nervous little hamsters
and you'll find out that babylon
is located in the vetmans garden
where maidens lay on cardboard pedestals
in elaborate wigs portraying lions
and the yawning abysses will shut their doors
and trolleybus number one will lower its poles
not holding hands, housekeepers
will head back from the matisa market
and army reservists will go out on the playgrounds
legs unsteady on the rubber soft-top
to distinguish fully the red swings
from the green slide, from the yellow horsey
and the vases on the opera house façade
will fill up with southern fruits, still warm
and beavers will perceive in their own tails
maris liepa's splayed foot
and the waters of the daugava will turn turquoise
for the edification of their numberless tributaries
and heads on the french embassy will turn
to see smoke belching from the opera house smoke-stack
and a climber will break through the thorns to the uppermost cables
and the last taxi will pull out from the chomsky bar
and bernard will at last put on a hat and coat
and lāčplēsha street will run straight and flat
and an anchorite will wander into berga bazaar
rattling his suitcase wheels on the paving stones
and some meatheads will get a black eye
from the girls at the entrance to the splendid palace
and the vacated tenants will whisper
more than they ought in the ears of cheated depositors
how fountains gush from dark canals
how people arrive tanned from warm southern countries
and the boosters will wipe the smiles from their faces
mistaking yet another supermarket for the train station
and the frozen river will be run over by the train
and then run over again by number two
and the stars will rise out of freedom's hands
and from the chasms a sunny drizzle will pour
and you and I will lay together on the lawn beneath the gingko
and try to lie completely still

* * *

быстро-быстро вынь из кармана, переложи в стакан
двигать не надо, рано, вообще не надо
а ты —
высунь язык и присядь
все нормально, ты к стойке и шел
шевелись, обходи, обходи
обойди кругом
выпростай руки, открой незаметно лицо
выдохни так, чтобы сиреневой краски
запах пошел изо рта
только пробка в руке так долго, что почти что вросла в ладонь
но руины отстроены заново, развалины заселены
все нормально, и тебе нашли замену тоже

INSTALLATION: TWO SONNETS

quickly pull it out of your pocket and put it in the glass
don't move, too soon, in general you shouldn't
and you –
stick out your tongue and squat
everything's OK, you were just going to the bar
move on, step along, step along
step on around
get your hand free, discreetly show your face
exhale so the lilac paint
smell comes out of your mouth
it's just you've held that cork so long it's nearly grown into your palm
but the ruins have been rebuilt, the wreckage is inhabited again
everything's OK, and there's already a replacement for you, too

* * *

стоя на краю могилы, на краю всех могил,
я обращаюсь от лица всех нестойких элементов,
от лица скособоченных и перелопаченных, и затертых,
от лица перепончатокрылых и обезличенных,
и от всех прочих лиц, и от лиц кавказской национальности,
и от своего поднадоевшего всем лица,
и от прочих органов и частей тела и вселенной,
я обращаюсь от лица и самим лицом,
обращаюсь настойчиво и в полный голос
ко всем свободным кустам и деревьям
ко всем жукам-тараканам, к ямам, ямочкам и ложбинкам,
ко всем, кто еще в силах держать свое маленькое
                  сморщенное оружие дулом вверх,
ко всем стручковым,
ко всему прогрессивному небосводу и собственно к горизонту:
товарищи! друзья! дамы и господа! маленькие собачки!
в эту минуту, когда глаза всего мира прикованы к биноклям,
когда руки всего человечества и работников
                  лесного хозяйства, и тети Сони,
      всех ершей с большой буквы
      всех карасей с маленькой
        и всех подлещиков с маленькой на большую
заняты только одним, самым полезным делом,
в эту минуту я обращаюсь к вам с призывом:
встаньте ровно!
поставьте ноги на ширину плеч!
положите всё на место!
прижмитесь горящим лбом к ночному стеклу!
и-раз, и-два, и-три, и-четыре,
и-раз, и-два, и-три, и-четыре!

* * *

не подумай, что это бездомный
просто он потерял ключи
и четвертый месяц ночует на ступеньках
мебельного магазина

кажется ему не очень удобно
в такой скрюченной позе
а на самом деле он акробат
и так ему намного сподручней дремать

с чего ты взяла, что он умер
подумаешь, не дышит
чего еще ждать от продвинутых йогов
умеющих задерживать дыхание на многие годы

ну, точнее, почти навсегда

PUBLICATION: SCHEMA

do not think he is homeless
he simply lost his keys
and for the past four months he's been sleeping
in front of a furniture store

you might think he's uncomfortable
all doubled up like that
in fact he's an acrobat
and finds this posture handy for dozing

what makes you think he's dead
so what if he isn't breathing
what else do you expect from a yoga master
who can hold their breath for years at a time,

almost forever, to be exact

* * *

зачем я так кричал, что я электрик
ведь не электрик я

что на меня нашло

показывал руками на розетки
и льнул к щитку, и счетчик обнимал

никто не верит

вот справки, видите, вот документы
из всех карманов провода торчат

молчат и смотрят

да в пять минут замкну любые клеммы
не остановишь как начну паять

что вы за люди

качают головой с сомненьем
ты нам не нужен, говорят

нам бы электрика

---

why did I keep yelling I'm an electrician
I'm no electrician

what came over me

I gestured at outlets
cosied up to the circuit box, held the meter close

no one is buying it

here's my license, look, my certificate
wires sticking out of all my pockets

they just look at me in silence

give me five minutes and I'll close any circuit
I'll get soldering you won't be able to stop me

what kind of people are you

they shake their heads doubtfully
we can't use you, they say

we need an electrician

***

когда в скафандре из очень чувствительной кожи
в состоянии полной невесомости
неподвижно лежишь на диване
и внутри всё запотевает от твоего дыхания
закрываешь глаза и слышишь как поют
за рекой, за оврагом, за лесом
будто поржавевшие диванные пружины
и ждёшь только одного: чтобы вместе
с короткой глубокой затяжкой в легкие
вошла почти забытая сила тяжести

PERFORMANCE: SLOW SHOW

when in a spacesuit of highly sensitive skin
in state of zero gravity
you lie motionless on the sofa
and everything within fogs up with your breathing
you shut your eyes you hear them singing
beyond the river, the gully, the forest
something like rusty sofa springs
and you wait for that thing:
that accompanied by an abrupt deep drag
the all-but-forgotten force of gravity enter your lungs

* * *

какие-то девы, скрывавшие девство свое — стюардессы? медсестры?
склонившись над ним, над раненым ветераном
шептали: ты ранен, мы кровь твою утираем
и они так бы и продолжали его вытирать
если бы он не воспротивился этому самым противоестественным образом
он умер — у них под руками
и они вытирали уже не его
а только лишь его плоть
своими пестрыми никому не нужными больше платьями, бесполезными отныне шелковыми платками

(тайком они любовались его противоестественным образом)

(не удивлюсь, кстати, если окажется, что он был болгарин вроде рудина или накануне)

СЕРГЕЙ ТИМОФЕЕВ

УТРО В СТРАНЕ ИНТРОВЕРТОВ

Негромко лает собака
на проезжающего на велосипеде.
Сдержанно портится погода
и рассыпается сарай.
Ночные птицы слегка критичны
по отношению к чудесам утра.
Солнце не может вспомнить,
до какой точки всходило вчера
и старается взять чуть ниже.
Дети просыпаются раньше всех
и читают свои книжки,
чтобы не будить взрослых.
Вода из крана льётся скромно,
не брызжет и почти сразу исчезает в стоке.
Еле-еле движутся тени ёлок и сосен.
Кто-то намазывает бутерброд тонким слоем масла.
По радио «Классика» передают интервью пианиста,
который на всё отвечает «да» или «нет».
Зато играет он очень точно,
с небольшими уверенными паузами.

MORNING IN A LAND OF INTROVERTS

A dog softly barks
at a passing cyclist.
With restraint, the weather grows worse
and the barn falls apart.
Night birds are slightly critical
of the glories of the morning.
The sun can't remember
to what point it ascended yesterday
and aims slightly lower.
Children rise before everyone else
and read their books
trying not to wake the grown-ups.
Water pours modestly from the tap
not splashing and disappearing in the drain almost at once.
Shadows of firs and pines barely move.
Someone spreads butter in a thin layer on bread.
The Classics radio station airs an interview with a pianist
who answers every question with "yes" or "no",
Although he plays very precisely,
with short, confident pauses.

ТИХИЙ БОГ

Мне некогда вспоминать, как я увидел
Тихого Бога, но если надо, я вам расскажу.
Я имею в виду – слушателям вашей программы...
Мы ехали с вечеринки, большой компанией, пять человек,
Я был за рулём, все остальные спали, перед этим

Провеселились всю ночь. Было огромное облачное утро
Повсюду, со всех сторон. Пышные кучерявые облака плыли
С какой-то новой силой, как будто газообразные животные,
Завидевшие своего хозяина и теперь изо всех сил
Стремящиеся подобраться поближе. Прямо над дорогой
Впереди я увидел пробивающиеся сквозь облака
Ровные струи света, они падали вниз торжественно
Как лучистые лестницы или как складки великолепной
Одежды. Невольно я засмотрелся, но как опытный водитель
Сбросил скорость и ехал не спеша, будто просто катился,
Вкатывался в это великолепие. Я чувствовал себя как зависший
Бильярдный шар, готовый через долю секунды опуститься
В грандиозную лунку. Я держал руль и улыбался, я был
Готов хохотать, но бесшумно. Струи света всё приближались,
И я понимал, что сейчас въеду прямо в них. Вокруг всё
Стало ярче в тысячу раз, и я увидел свои пальцы на руле,
Как никогда в жизни, они стали полупрозрачными и в них
Видны были жилки, косточки, нервы, они тоже светились,
Изнутри, как янтарь. И я закричал, что-то, не помню что.
Все проснулись мгновенно, думали что авария. А я кричал
И кричал – не мог остановиться, успел только затормозить,
И мои спутники вытащили меня из-за руля и повалили меня
На землю, и били меня по щекам, и лили на меня воду
Из пузатой пластиковой бутылки, и спрашивали: «Что
С тобой, ЧТО с тобой?» А я не мог ответить и только
Показывал на небо, откуда отвесно и непоправимо
Спускался Бог, прямо нам на головы. И тогда они
Наконец увидели и тоже закричали и бросились
Врассыпную, оставив меня на земле. И свет наконец
Стал ослепительным, а всё вокруг просто белым.
И я уже больше ничего не мог различить, всё
Было одного цвета, всё было из одного света, и я
Заплакал, потому что больше не мог кричать,
И потому что вокруг стояла такая тишина. И в этот
Момент Тихий Бог заговорил со мной, он сказал,

Чтобы я не пытался вскочить и броситься в сторону,
Он сказал: «Отдохни!» И я почувствовал, что свет
Лёг мне на лоб как рука. И я вспомнил себя в животе
У мамы и свернулся так же и лежал, пока свет шёл
Сквозь меня, словно колонны огромного невесомого храма,
А потом всё кончилось, а я всё ещё лежал и смотрел,
Как свет отступает, уходит, медленно и печально. Нет, я
Не пытался его удержать или догнать, но мне было
Так грустно, как бывает, когда смотришь – ты выиграл
В лотерею 25 тысяч, а потом поглядишь внимательней,
А это билет из прошлого розыгрыша, в общем – мимо,
И ты стоишь с ним в руке и думаешь: «Почему?!»
Вот и я стоял и думал так: «Почему?!» Через час примерно
Нашли меня опять мои спутники и без особых разговоров
Мы опять сели в машину и поехали. Потом вернулись в город,
Я всех развез по домам, приехал к себе и лёг спать.
Проснулся утром, был понедельник, я лежал, уткнувшись лицом
В подушку и ждал, но ничего особенного не происходило,
И тогда я встал, умылся и пошел на работу. Теперь
Каждые выходные я езжу по этой дороге взад и вперёд,
Но не вижу ни этих облаков, ни этого света. Я не могу сказать,
Что стал примерным христианином или кем-то еще.
Да и некогда там особенно думать, работы по горло,
Лето, самый сезон. Но когда меня пригласили на радио,
Дай, думаю, пойду, может я не один такой, может
Откликнется какой человек, по которому тоже
Прошёлся свет. И то было бы легче. Хотя не знаю,
О чём бы мы стали с ним говорить, так, может быть,
Помолчали бы вместе, пожали бы друг другу руки
И разошлись. Вот такая история. Но если с кем-то
Такое случится, не бойтесь, а потом... напишите мне,
Пожалуйста... Адрес в редакции. До свиданья!

INSTALLATION: GHOST OF THE BAKERY

QUIET GOD

I don't really have time to think back about how I saw
The Quiet God, but if you want, I can tell you about it.
I mean – your programme's listeners…
We were driving home from a bash, a fair number of us, five people.
I was at the wheel; everyone else was asleep.
We'd been partying all night. There was this huge, cloudy morning
Everywhere all around. Puffy, coiling clouds were rushing
With some kind of new-found force, like vaporous animals who,
Seeing their master, were giving their all
In an effort to get close to him. Right above the road
Ahead, piercing the clouds, I saw
Steady streams of light. They fell to earth magnificently,
Like radiant ladders or the folds of glorious
Clothing. I stared in unwilling fascination, but being an experienced driver,
Braked and continued at lower speed, as though I was just out for a ride.
Coasting into this gloriousness, I felt like a billiard ball, suspended,
Ready to descend in another fraction of a second
Into a marvellous corner pocket. I gripped the wheel and smiled. I was
Ready to laugh, but soundlessly. The streams of light kept getting closer,
And I saw that I was about to drive right into them. Everything around,
Got a thousand times brighter, and I saw my fingers on the wheel,
Like never before in my life – they were half-transparent and you could see
The veins, bones and nerves, and they were also shining
From inside, like amber. And I screamed something, I don't remember what.
Everyone woke up in an instant, thinking it was an accident, and I screamed
And screamed–I couldn't stop, but managed to step on the brakes.
And my friends pulled me out of the driver's seat and lay me
On the ground, and slapped my face, and poured water on me
From a tubby plastic bottle, and asked: "What's
Wrong? WHAT's wrong?" And I couldn't answer and just
Pointed at the sky, from where, vertically and irreversibly,
God was descending, right on our heads. Then they
Finally saw it and started screaming too and ran off
In all directions, leaving me there on the ground. And the light finally
Became blinding, and everything around turned white.
And I couldn't distinguish anything any more, everything
Was the same colour, everything was just made of light, and I
Started crying, because I couldn't scream any longer.
And because there was such quietness all around. And in that
Moment the Quiet God spoke with me, and told me
Not to try jumping up and running away;
He said, "Rest!" And I felt the light touch my forehead
Like a hand. And I remembered being in my mother's tummy
And I curled up like that and lay there, while the light
Went through me, like the columns of some enormous, weightless temple.
As the light pulls away, departs, slowly and sadly. No, I
Didn't try to hold on or chase after it, but I was
So sad, like when you look and see that you've won
Twenty-five thousand in the lottery, and then you look closer,
And the ticket's from the last draw – in general, no go.
And you stand there with it in your hand and think, "Why?"
And I stood there like that and thought, "Why?!" In about an hour
My friends found me again and without saying much
We got in the car and drove on. We got back to the city.
I drove everyone home, I got to my own place and went to bed.
Woke up in the morning, it was Monday; and I lay face down
On the pillow and waited, but nothing special was happening;
So I got up, showered and went to work. Now
Every weekend I drive back and forth along that road,
But I never see those clouds or that light, I can't say
That I've become a model Christian or anything else.
And there's no time to think about it anyway, with work up to here –
It's summer, height of the season. But when you invited me on the radio
I thought, OK, I'll go, maybe I'm not the only one,
Maybe I'll get a response from someone else
The light has gone through. Maybe then it would be a bit easier.
But I don't know what we'd talk about, and so maybe
We'd just be quiet together, would shake hands,
And then go our separate ways. So that's the story.
But if something like this happens to someone else,
Don't be afraid. And afterwards… write to me.
Please… The office has the address. Goodbye!

ЕЁ НЕФТЬ

Из коленных чашечек у неё идёт нефть,
Колени сочатся нефтью.
В хороший день можно набрать
Полулитровую банку,
Если водить её краешком по коже,
Цепляя маслянистые капли.
И что с этим делать?
Врачи только собирают консилиумы,
Хорошо хоть не раструбили журналистам.
Родные уже привыкли к тому,
Что она ходит всё время в чёрных тугих
Лосинах со специальными уплотнениями
На коленях, впитывающими всё новые капли.
Нефть – это её повседневность,
Она даже отслеживает курс на неё,
Колебания рынка, как чей-то пульс,
Чуть лихорадочный, переменный, живой,
Непонятный. В последнее время
Она чувствует себя целой
Нефтедобывающей страной.
Государством, уверенным в своём смысле.
Смотрите, как она переходит улицу,
Как смеётся, как делает покупки.
Ничего, что от нефти она избавляется
В ванной, снова и снова смывая тяжёлые
Чёрные капли. У неё в этой жизни
Есть нефть. А что есть у вас?

HER OIL

Oil comes out of her kneecaps.
Her knees are oozing with oil.
On a good day you can accumulate
A half-litre bottle,
By dragging the lip along her skin,
Catching unctuous drops.
And what can you do about that?
The doctors just hold consultations;
At least they haven't sounded off to the press.
Her relatives are already used to her
Always wearing those snug black
Leggings with special padding
On the knees to soak up all the droplets.
Oil is her daily routine.
She even keeps an eye on prices,
Market fluctuations, like someone's pulse,
Slightly feverish, dynamic, alive,
And unfathomable. Lately
She feels like she's a whole
Oil-producing nation herself–
A state, confident of its own significance.
Look how she crosses the street,
How she laughs, goes shopping.
So what if she gets rid of the oil
In the bath, wiping away heavy black drops
Again and again. In this life of ours
She has oil. What have you got?

СИСТЕМА В СИСТЕМЕ

Он работал в ФБР в группе захвата, десять лет, прежде чем положил рапорт об отставке на стол начальника. Никаких логических причин для подобного шага он не мог привести. Отдел контроля личного состава, изучив вопрос, решил отправить его на закрытое психологическое освидетельствование. Он прошёл череду бесед с местными психологами, и вот что выяснилось. Дальше следует расшифрованная запись беседы от 15 февраля. Он говорит: «…После захвата мы обычно обыскивали квартиры на предмет оружия, наркотиков и улик. Заглядывали во все углы. И вот что я стал замечать – каждый раз когда я открывал холодильник, на верхней полке стоял персиковый йогурт в уже приоткрытой упаковке, наполовину опустошённый. А рядом лежали два перезрелых банана. Я обратил на это внимание в 2010-м, когда мы брали одного типа в Вашингтоне, в том же году это повторилось в Денвере, потом в Канзас-сити, и пошло-поехало. В конечном счёте я обнаружил 15 холодильников по всей стране именно с таким набором предметов на верхней полке. Но что меня доконало – это последний случай в Нью-Йорке: в квартире был огромный белый холодильник. На верхней полке снова была полупустая упаковка персикового йогурта. Но рядом лежали три! перезрелых банана. Я подумал – что за ерунда! Т.е. я и раньше так думал. Но это меня добило. И в системе – никакой системы, понимаете? И в системе – никакой системы…» Резолюция начальника отдела: «Поздравить опрошенного с переходом на новый уровень. Присвоить ему доступ ND, перевести под контроль службы предотвращения невозможного с повышением оклада и страховых выплат. Вернуть к исполнению служебных обязанностей».

THE SYSTEM IN THE SYSTEM

He worked in the FBI strike force for ten years, then placed a letter of resignation on his superior's desk. He couldn't articulate a single logical reason for this step. The personnel division, on consideration, decided to send him for a confidential psychological evaluation. He sat through a string of interviews with in-house psychologists, leading to the following conclusions. What follows is a decoded transcript of the February 15 interview. He says: "... After a strike we usually searched the premises for weapons, narcotics and other evidence. Looking in every crack, I began to notice: every time I opened a refrigerator, on the top shelf there was a peach yoghurt with an open lid, half eaten. Next to it there were always two overripe bananas. This came to my attention in 2010, while capturing a suspect in Washington, in the same year it happened again in Denver, then in Kansas City, and then it really took off. Ultimately, I discovered fifteen refrigerators across the entire country with precisely this combination of items on the top shelf. But the final straw was that last time in New York: the apartment had a huge, white refrigerator. On the top shelf, once again, a half-empty container of peach yoghurt. But next to it were three (!) overripe bananas. I thought – what the hell! That is, I thought the same thing earlier. But this was too much. Even in the system there's no system, get it? No system in the system...." The verdict of the division chief: "Congratulate the subject with advancement to the next level. Grant him clearance for ND; transfer him under the authority of division for prevention of impossibilities with increase in salary and enhanced benefits. Return to fulfilment of assigned duties."

PERFORMANCE: BERLIN PANDA THEATRE

INSTALLATION: RIGHT, KINETIC POEM

ЖУЧКИ, ВЕТОЧКИ

«Я стал плохим человеком,
всюду вижу плохое», –
сказал мне пассажир
междугороднего автобуса
в ходе негромкого ночного разговора.
«В деревьях вижу жучков,
в поэзии – тавтологию,
в речах политиков – речи политиков.
Может быть, это не навсегда,
и когда-нибудь я снова увижу
в деревьях – изящество веток,
в поэзии – щедрость оттенков,
в речах политиков – варианты будущего.
Но пока – как стена. Сами понимаете,
это только мои проблемы. Мир ведь
по-прежнему абсолютно, абсолютно
прекрасен…» И он умолк, глядя в окно
на уплывающий назад среди тьмы
одинокий дом с парой горящих окон,
где, видимо, смотрели сериал
под конфеты и крепкий чай.

BUGS, BOUGHS

"I've become a bad person –
everywhere I see bad things,"
said a passenger
in an intercity bus to me
in the course of a hushed evening conversation.
"In the trees I see bugs;
in poetry – tautology;
in politicians' speeches – politicians' speeches.
Maybe it won't last forever,
and some day I'll again see
in the trees – elegance of boughs;
in poetry – generosity of nuance;
in politicians' speeches – alternatives for the future.
But for now it's like a wall. You understand,
it's just my problem. The world
is still absolutely, absolutely
magnificent." And he fell silent, looking out the window
at a house, slipping away into the dark,
with a pair of lit windows,
where they were watching a TV show, it seems,
with chocolates and strong tea.

ПРОГНОЗ

Уже 10 лет назад я говорил тебе,
Что это навсегда – эти деревья, эти поля, эти неудачи,
Эти скромные неуверенные победы,
Эти придорожные кафе, торгующие пустым воздухом
И немодной музыкой,
Эти дни, когда родители приводят своих детей
В первый раз в школу,
Испытывая щемящую смесь тревоги и радости,
Эти яблоки, этот туман по утрам в низинах,
Этот консервированный горошек, украшающий
Главный салат страны.
А ты говорил про шоппинг-молы отсюда до горизонта,
Стопки глянцевых журналов прямо у порога,
Бесконечные шестиполосные шоссе,
Утыкающиеся прямо в море,
Ночи, переходящие в дни,
Как одна твёрдая валюта – в другую.
И где это всё? Спрашиваю тебя об этом
На автобусной остановке,
Украшенной скромным объявлением
О пропаже двух такс, девочек, чёрного окраса.
Оно распечатано на принтере
Позавчера.

FORECAST

It's been ten years since I told you
That it's forever: these trees, these fields, these misfortunes,
These modest, timid successes,
These roadside cafes, peddling vacant air
And unfashionable music,
These days, when parents bring their kids
To school for the first time,
Feeling a wrenching mix of anxiety and joy:
These apples, this morning fog in the gullies,
These canned peas, glory
Of the national salad.
And you spoke of shopping malls from here to the horizon,
Stacks of glossy magazines right by the door,
Endless six-lane highways,
Driving right into the sea,
Nights that pass into days
Like one hard currency into another.
And where is all that? I ask you
At a bus stop,
Decorated with a simple announcement
Of the loss of two Dachshunds, female, with dark coloration.
It was generated on a printer
Two days ago.

БОСИКОМ

Я помню эту девушку,
Мы работали вместе в рекламном агентстве,
И там всюду на полу был серый ковролин,
По которому в то жаркое лето она бродила босиком,
Раздавая нам какие-то задания:
То рекламировать детские сухие смеси, то
Европейский Союз, то марку машин, чьё название
На нашем языке звучало почти один в один как cunt.
Там был даже свой душ,
Которым пользовались макетировщики,
Заявлявшиеся на работу с бодуна.
А офис этот располагался на улице,
Чьё название (снова незадача)
На языке соседней страны воспринималось как «задница»,
И здесь частенько можно было повстречать туристов
Именно оттуда, радостно скалящихся и делающих селфи
На фоне табличек на угловых домах.
Вот такая у них была наивная чистая радость.
И так это и было, лето, солнечное утро
И стайка иностранцев, широко улыбающихся
В маленькие глазки фотомыльниц на ближайшем углу.
Вообще хорошее было местечко,
Непафосное, несмотря на род занятий,
И, наверное поэтому, хотя и
Это наше агентство три раза меняло
 своё название
(Одно загадочнее и невзрачнее
 другого),
Оно всё-таки вылетело в трубу.
Но я помню ту девушку, как она
Ходила по серому ковролину среди
 мониторов,
Столов, заваленных бумагами и
 чашками из-под кофе,
В своём цветастом платье.
Просто дух захватывало.
Босиком.

BAREFOOT

I remember that girl,
We worked together in an ad agency
With grey wall-to-wall carpet on the floors,
And that hot summer she would wander across it barefoot
Giving us various assignments:
Either advertising for baby formula, or
For the European Union, or for a car brand, with a name
That in our language sounded almost exactly like "cunt".
There was even a shower there,
That the lay-out guys would use
When they showed up to work with a hangover.
And this office was located on a street,
With a name (another problematic case)
That in a neighbouring country's language could be taken for "ass",
And you would frequently run into tourists there
From that country, grinning in glee and taking selfies
Against the background of street signs posted at the corners.
That was a pure, naïve joy they had
And that's the way it was. Summer, a sunny morning
Packs of tourists, smiling broadly
Into the lenses of disposable cameras on the corner nearby.
It was a fine place, in general,
Low key, despite the line of work,
And, probably for just that reason, even though
Our agency changed its name three times
(Each name more mysterious and obscure than the last),
It went up in smoke all the same.
But I remember that girl, how she
Would walk over the grey carpeting among the monitors,
Tables piled high with papers and coffee cups,
In her flower-print dress.
It just took your breath away.
Barefoot.

ПОПУЛЯРНАЯ МЕЛОДИЯ ДЛЯ УКУЛЕЛЕ

Напиши мне роман,
В котором будет идти речь о другом романе,
Всё равно не прочитаю ни первый, ни второй –
Я уеду в Маньчжурию и сгину ни за что.

Нарисуй мне картину, на которой будет
Изображена другая картина,
Всё равно я не увижу ни той, ни другой –
Я уеду в Маньчжурию и сгину ни за что.

Сочини мне песню, в которой будут слова
О совсем другой песне,
Всё равно я не услышу ни одну, ни другую –
Я уеду в Маньчжурию и сгину ни за что

ЧТО-ТО ВРОДЕ ДОКЛАДА

Кошка – ночное животное,
Бегает по дому и говорит по-испански,
При каждой возможности протирает стол,
Вообще похожа на снегоуборочную машину,
Оставленную без присмотра с работающим мотором.
Она была здесь и в прошлом году, я слышал,
Как она перешагивала предметы, кружила под
Диванами, заметала следы хвостом. И теперь
Она здесь, и в глазах её читается немой вопрос:
«Как звали капитана турецкой футбольной сборной
1951-го года?» Я мог бы включить компьютер
И найти ответ. Но за ним потянется ещё цепочка
Вопросительных знаков. И это будет больше похоже
На допрос. Поэтому я откупаюсь сухим кормом
И мисочкой воды. Изображаю из себя хозяина.
А она засыпает под утро, пройдя тысячу дорог,
Посетив тысячу мест, вымолив прощение.

SOMETHING LIKE A REPORT

The cat, a nocturnal animal,
Runs around the house and talks in Spanish
Wipes the table at every opportunity,
In general, resembles a snow plough,
Left unattended with engine running.
She was here last year, too, I heard her,
How she stepped around objects, did circles under
The sofas, sweeping tracks away with her tail. And now
She's here, and you can read a mute question in her eyes:
"What was the name of the Turkish all-star football team captain
In 1951?" I could turn on the computer
And find the answer. But a whole chain of question marks
Would follow. And that would start looking more like
An interrogation. So I buy myself off with dry food
And a little bowl of water. Pretend to be her owner.
She falls asleep at dawn, having travelled a thousand roads,
Visited a thousand places, begged and received absolution.

ОТЕЛЬ РИТЦ

Выложенный голубой мозаикой
С путеводными звездами пол
SPA-бассейна и продуманная подсветка
Вместе с шумом струящейся воды,
Как будто вечно догоняющей саму себя,
Настраивают на философский тон. Сейчас
Полдень и здесь никого нет, только где-то
В глубине за стеклами мелькает тень
Черноволосой женщины в белом, проверяющей
По-прежнему ли достаточно кристально чистых полотенец
И банных халатов. Их – более чем. Высокие
Полки до потолка выложены свёрнутыми
Вафельными рулонами. В то же время они
Лежат не вплотную, вокруг каждого есть пространство,
Ведь и посетители здесь – штучный товар.
Выбравшись из джакузи и насухо вытершись,
Ты надеваешь халат, застегиваешь его,
Вставляешь ноги в белые махровые тапочки,
И проходишь мимо кожаных лежанок и
Зала для занятий спортом, мимо стеклянных
Полок с разной ерундой для тела и выходишь
К зеркалам и лифту. Раскрываются двери,
Ты вставляешь свою карточку и нажимаешь кнопку
Этажа. Ты живешь на восьмом. 808. Как будто
Зацикленный между двумя бесконечностями. Ты – потерянный
Участник конференции по сотрудничеству. Компьютер дал сбой
И тебя не выписывают уже третью неделю. Посещаешь
Завтраки, где у тебя есть свой столик, и оставляешь
В номере конфетки уборщицам, молодым светловолосым
Девушкам, отчаянно вежливым и педантичным. Обильного
Завтрака хватает на целый день, а вечером можно перехватить
Кебаб, а потом пойти погонять зайцев на лужайках огромного
Парка. В это время его пересекают почти исключительно
Велосипедисты. Спишь ты хорошо, с закрытыми окнами и
Включенным кондиционером. Когда они наконец обнаружат
Ошибку, то скорее всего тебе удастся скрыться и лечь на дно.
Лишь бы там была голубая мозаика.

PERFORMANCE: PLACE USA

THE RITZ

Inlaid with a blue mosaic showing
The lode stars, the floor
Of the spa-bath and the circumspect illumination
Along with the sound of running water,
As though in eternal pursuit of itself,
Puts you in a philosophical mood. Now it's
Midday and no one is around, except somewhere
In the depths behind the glass a shadow flits by
Of a dark-haired woman in white, checking
Whether there are still enough snow-white towels
And bath robes. There are more than enough. The tall
Shelves, reaching to the ceiling, are piled with rolled-up
Waffle-textured bundles. All the same, they
Don't lie close together, each has space around it,
And, just as surely, the guests here are one-offs.
After rising out of the Jacuzzi and wiping yourself dry,
You put on a robe, tie the belt,
Stick your feet in white, terry-towel slippers,
And walk past the leather chaise-longues and
The sports facility, past the glass
Shelves with various body products, to come out
By the mirrors near the elevators. The doors open,
You insert your card and press the button
For your floor. You are on the eighth. 808. As though
Caught between two infinitudes. You are a lost
Participant from the conference on partnership. Due to a computer glitch
It's been three weeks and they haven't checked you out yet. You go to
The breakfast, where you have your own table, and leave
Chocolates in the room for the maids, young fair-haired
Girls, hopelessly polite and pedantic. The abundant
Breakfast is enough to last you all day, and in the evening you can grab
A kebab, and then chase rabbits on the lawns of the huge
Park. By this hour it's being criss-crossed almost exclusively
By cyclists. You sleep well, with closed windows and
The AC turned on. When they at last discover
Their mistake, you'll probably be able to hide and lie low in the depths.
So long as there is that blue mosaic.

ПОСТКОММУНИКАЦИЯ

Свяжитесь с нами,
оплатите услуги,
примите наши поздравления,
окажите нам доверие.
Распечатайте это на досуге,
пересчитайте ставку,
распределите напряжение
на сеть,
окружите окружность.
И вот ещё что.
В данный момент
все операторы заняты.
Значит ли это, что уже в следующий –
они свободны и счастливы?
Богаты и успешны?
Независимы и спокойны?

POSTCOMMUNICATION

Contact us,
pay for services,
accept our congratulations,
place your faith in us.
Print this out at your leisure,
recalculate your rate,
distribute current
in the network,
surround the roundness.
And one more thing.
At the present moment
all operators are busy.
Does this mean that at the next –
they'll be free and happy?
prosperous and successful?
Independent and tranquil?

ФИГУРЫ РЕЧИ

Трогательный, наивный, какой-то искренний
Истребитель пролетел над речкой. Спелый
Напомаженный танк уютно перебирал гусеницами,
Подъезжая к лесу. Заветно, по-детски бабахнула
Установка залпового огня. Счастливые довольные
Пехотинцы куда-то побежали. В небе росли
Дымчатые раскрывающиеся цветки взрывов.
Небольшой коренастый генерал обещал
Взять всё, что можно, до полуночи. Весёлый
Озорной корреспондент держал перед ним
Микрофон с номером канала. Телезрители
Радовались и блаженно отдувались от трансляции.
Мыльная война пенилась перед ними во всём
Своём маслянистом блеске. Сверкало солнце.

FIGURES OF SPEECH

The touching, naive, somehow sincere
Fighter jet flew over the river. The ripe,
Pomaded tank cosily set its treads down,
Approaching the woods. Intimately, childishly, a thump
Was heard from the salvo fire system. Happy, contented
Infantrymen ran off somewhere. Growing in the sky were
Smoky, blooming flowers of explosions.
A slight, stubby general promised
To seize everything possible by midnight. The happy
Mischievous correspondent held before him
A microphone with the number of his channel. TV-viewers
Rejoiced and puffed up in bliss at the broadcast.
The soapy war foamed up before them in all
Its unctuous lustre. The sun shimmered.

ВОПРОСЫ

Достаточно ли мы держали в ладонях ежевики, морошки, клюквы? Не подозрительно ли много попадалось нам незрелых ягод или, наоборот, уже слегка подвяленных, с коричневыми бочками? Ступали ли мы мягко по коврам августовских лесов? Зажигали ли фонарики в самое тёмное время суток? Работали ли на лесопилках молчаливыми загадочными фигурами, утирающими пот? Спали ли на пригорках, разметав руки? Становились ли постепенно примерами неразборчивого неаккуратного почерка? Оставляли ли отпечатки ладоней в прибрежном песке у неспешной речки? Расцепляли ли не поддающиеся тугие ветки? Хорошо ли мы прожили жизнь до сегодняшнего момента? Всегда ли мы были правы? Не пропустили ли что-то важное?

ЭКСКУРСИИ

Все печальные джинсы 70-х
(не путать со счастливыми джинсами 60-х
и бесшабашными джинсами 50-х)
завязали в один узел
и упрятали в заброшенный карьер
где-то под Питтсбургом.
Туда даже иногда привозят экскурсии
из близлежащих школ.
«Почему джинсы — печальные?» — спрашивают дети.
«Мы не знаем», — отвечают учителя.
«Мы только догадываемся», — говорят учителя.
«Мы плохо помним», — признаются учителя.

FIELD TRIPS

All the sad jeans of the seventies
(not to be confused with the happy jeans of the sixties,
or the rowdy jeans of the fifties)
were tied up in a single bundle
and confined in an abandoned quarry
somewhere near Pittsburgh.
Once in a while they even bring in field-trips
from nearby schools.
"Why are the jeans sad?" ask the children.
"We don't know," answer the teachers.
"We can only guess," say the teachers.
"We can't really remember," admit the teachers.

ВЛАДИМИР СВЕТЛОВ

* * *

на avenu авеню
после конца света
над случайно спасшимися
в бетонной клетке
лежали на полу
в пробоину окна
холодный ветер
задувал снежинки
но холод
не преграда
лишенным тела адресатам
холод нипочем
нас согревают
искр касанья
электричество
нам заменяет жизнь
сигнал
накопленный заряд
цепочка да-да-нет
вспышка
отблеск
тишина

on avenu avenue
after the end of the world
above the accidental survivors
in the concrete cell
they lay on the floor
in the window embrasure
a cold wind
drove snowflakes
but the cold
is no barrier
to addressees lacking bodies
the cold as easy as pie
we're warmed up
by sparks of contact
of electricity
our lives superseded
by a signal
an accumulated charge
the string yes-yes-no
flash
glimmer
silence

* * *

от этой нашей нежности

все трещит по швам и сыплется
портной наготове услужливо

держит шелк и ножницы

то зашиваешь, то режешься

пальцы все исколоты

мечешься, материшься, хорохоришься
врешь-правду-режешь

и снова колешься

заговорщически подмигиваешь
неизвестно кому улыбаешься

после долгого сна тревожного

не наспишься, не напросыпаешься

from this our tenderness
everything bursts at the seams and spills out
the tailor obligingly at the ready
holds silk and scissors
now you sew, now cut yourself
fingers all pricked
you rush around, curse, get huffy
lie-truth-cut
and prick yourself again
wink conspiratorially
smile at who knows who
after a long disturbed sleep
can't get rested can't wake up

* * *

что скажешь?

что ты скажешь
когда придет день
вечеринка и ночь закончатся
развлечения и радость
закончатся
все закончится
целиком
что ты скажешь?

как и он думал
что слишком много любви
слишком
слишком много любви
слишком
воспоминания
которые удержать на ночь
ни больше
ни дольше

в комнате не убрано

PUBLICATION: ORBITA 5

what'll you say?

what will you say
when the day comes
party and night will end
fun and happiness
will end
everything will end
wholly
what will you say?

just as he thought
that there's too much love
too much
too much love
too much
memories
detaining for a night
no more
no longer

room's a mess

* * *

давай уйдем туда, где нас застали
закончим там, где нас нашли

в обратной перемотке
прикосновений рук и губ

снимаем поцелуй и забываем

вкус губ, движенье рук, изгиб спины
совсем не помню, как тебя зовут
мы станем одевать друг друга
так нежно, как никто не одевал
застежки, пуговицы, всё ли на местах?
вдруг в лифте исчезает запах

не успели до такси, сначала чаевые
официантке наплевать и так

кофе дерьмовый, дальше не помню…
кто эта девушка?!?!?!?

let's depart for where they caught us
we'll finish where they found us

in a rewind of
the touch of hands and lips

we'll steal that kiss and forget

taste of lips, hand movements, back's arch
don't remember your name at all
we'll start dressing one another
more tenderly than anyone has ever dressed
buckles, buttons, all in place?
suddenly in the elevator the scent vanishes
almost got to taxi, but first the tip
it's all the same to the waitress
crappy coffee, after that I don't remember…
who is that girl?!?!?!?

КРАСИВОЕ

человек путается на грани кожи
где кончается свет

запах искусственного меха
чувствуется
если

идти вслед отставая на полшага

его доносит воздух

движенье

уже от того возникающее

что идут два человека

так

можно

обращать внимание на тех

которые считают красивое – похожим
носят одинаковые подошвы

и цвет губ выбирают не для себя

но можно

искать других

но и они

непохожие

похожи на других таких же непохожих
так что красота становится
делом случайного выбора

THE BEAUTIFUL

people flounder at skin's edge
where light ends

the scent of artificial fur
is sensed
if

one follows a half-step behind

it is brought by air

a movement

which arises simply

because two people are walking

so

one may

turn attention to those

who consider the beautiful to be the similar
they wear identical soles

and pick out lip colour for others
but one may

seek out others

yet even they

are dissimilar

similar to others just as dissimilar
and so beauty becomes
a matter of random choice

* * *

скажи «изюм» детка
и сладко станет
кончик языка
мне покажи чуть-чуть
твое тело зовет, твое тело манит
твое тело плачет
ты маленькая конфетка детка
ты леденец прохладной сладости
в уголках губ
смысл твоих объятий прост
люби меня детка, люби
и пафосно так, на низких
животом пропоет
моя жизнь – клубок
развернешь нитью
свернешь
не найдешь

INSTALLATION: POWER INDEPENDENT POETRY

say "raisin," baby
and it'll get sweet
the tip of your tongue –
show it to me just a bit
your body calls, your body beckons
your body weeps
you little candy baby
you lollipop of cool sweetness
in the corners of your lips
the meaning of your embraces is simple,
love me, baby, love
and with pathos, in low tones
sung from the stomach
my life – a tangle
unwind its threads
and roll it up
not to be found again

КОНФИДЕНЦИАЛЬНЫЙ РАЗГОВОР

не знаю почему он начал этот разговор

и назвал его конфиденциальным

я подобрал его на шоссе

радиоприемник машины раздирали
истеричные синтезаторы и гитары восьмидесятых
начал загадочно поэтично про поцелуи в тени сомнений
будто он шпионил за мной
и прятал свои открытия в тетрадях
он шпионил за мной, но хотел признаться
менял лица, не подходил близко
еще странная майка на нем была
сильно застиранная
лучшие девушки
мертвые девушки
было написано
они никогда
не говорят нет
а потом опять за свое, про
золотые блики на черной воде
говорит надо
уйти под них
и смотреть изнутри
на
золотые блики на черной воде

больше я его никогда не видел
выходя крикнул что бросит камень
в лобовое стекло
не веришь?
кричал

я был спокоен
не знаю почему

CONFIDENTIAL CONVERSATION

i don't know why he began that conversation
and called it confidential
i picked him up on the highway
the car radio was being torn apart
by hysterical synthesizers and guitars from the eighties
he began mysteriously poetically about kisses in the shadow of doubts
as though he were spying on me
and concealing his discoveries in notebooks
he was spying on me, but wanted to confess
changed his expression, didn't come near
and he was in a strange t-shirt
extremely washed out
the best girls
are dead girls
was written on it
they never
say no
and then he started off again, about
golden flecks on the black water
he says gotta
get beneath them
and look from inside
at
golden flecks on the black water

i never saw him again after that
as he got out he screamed he'd throw a rock
through my windscreen
don't believe me?
he screamed
i was calm
don't know why

КЛИК, КЛИК

клик, клик
я снимаю костлявых моделей для бука
клик, клик
я танцую с министром регионального развития
для обложки
клик, клик
я снимаю молодого парня
для рубрики секс услуги
клик, клик
он любит маленьких животных,
и хочет стать ветеринаром
в этом большом зоосаде
большие животные
нравятся сельским парням
коровы, свиньи, лошади
а ему нравятся маленькие,
так что если наша собачка заболеет
я знаю к кому обращаться.
клик, клик
а недавно видел диких лошадей
вот странное зрелище!
клик, клик
нет существа бессмысленней,
это не про них, что пасутся вдали
и уносятся быстрее ветра
если подойти ближе
не чужды человеческой ласки
тоже в основе своей сексуальной,
весь день жрут на месте,
и заигрывают с кобылами
а если осталась во лбу звездочка
от селектированных предков,
то может и не возьмут в стадо
другую лошадь
клик, клик
есть еще дикая корова в том заповеднике
только ушла куда-то
клик, клик

click, click
I shoot emaciated models for a tome
click, click
I dance with the minister of regional development
for a cover
click, click
I shoot a young guy
for the sex services pages header
click, click
he likes small animals
and wants to become a vet
for this big zoo
rural guys
like large animals
cows, pigs, horses
but he likes small ones
so if our little dog gets sick
I know who to go to.
click, click
recently I saw some wild horses
what a strange sight!
click, click
they're the most pointless creatures
I don't mean the ones that graze in the distance
and run off faster than the wind
if you come up close
they're not averse to the human caress
also sexual in nature,
all day they chomp away in one place,
and cavort with the foals
but if a star shows up on the forehead
from crossbred ancestors
then they might not accept a given horse
into the herd
click, click
there's also a wild cow in that preserve
but it wandered off somewhere
click, click

ХИТ-ПАРАД

словно подарок за доверие
постоянным клиентам
нам даны эти дни
дни счастья
улыбок и понимающих взглядов
дни ангелов поющих звучно трубами
с чуть озверевшими от презрения глазами
нас есть за что презирать
и за что нам перерезать глотку тоже есть
нас есть в чем обвинить
но ангелы в алмазных доспехах
сияют даже в пасмурные дни
их песня не смолкает…
вот чем я действительно хотел бы заняться
так это провести остаток дней
составляя хит-парад
100 лучших песен
всех времен и народов

HIT PARADE

like a gift for loyalty
to repeat customers
we have been given these days
days of happiness
of smiles and understanding glances
days of angels singing resonantly with horns
with eyes slightly feral from derision
there's reason enough to despise us
and also to slice our throats
there's plenty we can be accused of
but angels in their armour of diamonds
shine even on cloudy days
their songs never fall silent…
now that's what I'd really like to do
to spend the rest of my days
composing a hit-parade
of the 100 best songs
of all times and nations

ДЕНЬГИ

посредник неудачный
в вечной гонке
потока красоты к деньгам
тебе не устоять –
снесет
напрасно
цепляешься
говоришь что деньги
не проблема
если деньги есть
и каждый раз
ты будешь замирать
нащупывать как пульс
бумажник
изрядно
потерявший в толщине
чтобы холодными руками
на последние монеты
еще одно желанье променять
и если б девушка моя
была деньгами
любил бы больше

ONLINE PROJECTS

MONEY

hapless middleman
in the eternal race
the flow of beauty towards money –
no way to resist
it'll wash you away
you hang on
say money
in futility
is no problem
if there's money
and every time
you freeze in place
groping, like for a pulse
at your wallet
severely
diminished in thickness
so that with cold hands
you can exchange your last coins
for one more wish
and if my girl
were money
you'd like her more

ПУСТОЙ АЭРОПОРТ

пустой аэропорт
самолеты
спят
пастор забирает с таможни белых голубей
святой дух для шоу в парке
возбужденные пудели общаются по дороге к такси
цирковое представление
для ловли доверчивых душ
ты делаешь несколько моментальных снимков
бар ночью закрыт
открыта церковь
в аэропорту
бетон и дерево
не помню архитектора
приз прошлого года
мы едем дальше
к морю
деревья еще с листьями
подсвечены фонарями снизу
отраженным от асфальта черным цветом
море густое как нефть
застывает перед нами
как наивны заигрывания человека с морем
все эти лодки рыбаков
купания у берега летом
что там?
в этой черной
выталкивающей нас массе
хочется отойти подальше
быстрее
мы идем по ночной юрмале
в надежде что хоть в одном кафе
не спит бармен
но напрасно

EMPTY AIRPORT

empty airport
planes
sleeping
a pastor picks up white doves at customs
the holy spirit here for a show in the park
excited poodles hobnob on the way to the taxi
a circus show
to catch trusting souls
you take some instant photos
the bar is closed at night
the church is open
in the airport
concrete and wood
can't recall the architect
a prize last year
we drive on
to the sea
trees still have leaves
lit by street lamps from below
with black light reflected from the asphalt
sea thick like oil
becomes motionless before us
flirtations of man with sea are so naive
all these fishing boats
and bathing at the shore in summer
what is it?
in this black
mass that repulses us
a desire to get as far away as possible
quickly
we walk through nighttime jūrmala
in hopes that in at least one café
the bartender is awake
but in vain

ОДНОКЛАССНИК

хорошие были времена,
но коммуникация сложная
вместо фейсбука носили пачку фотографий с собой
с интимными моментами
в ушах плеер,
давали друг другу послушать
если нравилось,
просили переписать
теперь
обсуждаем
искренни ли были официанты?
когда улыбались,
или их заставляют?
и они улыбаются через силу?
вот эти вот
молодые,
красивые
которые тратят на имидж больше чем на жизнь
 долго бредут по болотной грязи
чтобы сделать один снимок у реки в чистых костюмах

тогда кино и звезды были реальными,
если мерцали, то никто не знал
кроме друзей и близких

геи тогда еще хотели были удочерены
то Мадонной, то Тори Эймос
через одного

так и закончилась история

без детей в первом классе
с адаптированными родителями
вот и парижане теперь кажется помнят
как Бенджамин Клементин пел в метро и на улице.
а где кстати теперь тот парень,
помнишь?
который переплывал реки,
переходил границы,
чтобы пешком дойти до Парижа,
пока его снова не депортируют?
закрытые ночью скверы,

теперь понятно почему,
похоже и у нас скоро тоже так будет
говорит

еще говорит
одна девушка рассказывала
про ужас жизни в многодетной семье
утром не найти свои вещи
уже кто-то по ошибке принял за свои.

ты заметил, что мы используем слово рассказывать про
заметки в Фб?

INSTALLATION: ACTUAL SPACESCAPE

CLASSMATE

it was good times,
but communications were complicated
instead of facebook people carried around packs of photos
of personal moments
walkman playing in the ears,
they would pass it around to listen
if they liked something
would ask to make a recording
now
we discuss
whether those waiters were sincere
when they smiled
or are they forced to do that?
and they're making this huge effort to smile?
and take those
young
beautiful people
who spend more on their image than on life
to get a single shot by the river in a clean suit
wandering forever through swamp mud
back then movies and the stars were the real thing
if they twinkled, no one knew
except their friends and family
gays still wanted to get adopted
by Madonna, and then by Tori Amos
alternately
and that's how the story ended
without kids in first grade
with adopted parents
it seems like now the Parisians remember
how Benjamin Clementine sang in the metro and on the street
and by the way where is that guy now,
remember?
who swam through rivers,
crossed borders
to get to Paris on foot,
before they could deport him again?
the squares are closed at night,
now it's clear why,
and it seems it'll be like that here soon, too,
he says
and he also says
one girl told all about
the horror of life in a family with multiple kids
can't find your things in the morning
someone's already mistaken them for their own.
have you noticed we use the word "to tell" about
posts in FB?

АРТУР ПУНТЕ

***

Дорожка к его камню на высокой дюне
идет через прозрачный сосновый лес
высокий, прямой, мигающий солнцем в верхушках
словно празднующий тысячелетия отступления моря
но "мы здесь пробираемся как будто на ощупь
ночью в коридорах квартиры
с клеем-пистолетом в руке, опасаясь наступить
на брошенную игрушку,
изображающую фильтр пылесоса"
вот что это напоминает, говоришь ты
а мне и сказать нечего
какое-то время мы тихо стоим над камнем с фотографией
пока ты снова находишь нужные слова
"А ведь однажды мы целовались с ним
после концерта". Что тут добавить?
"Могу подбросить обратно"
Долго молча вести машину, это то, что я умею

INSTALLATION: OBJECT NO. 1

The path to his stone on the high dune
leads through an airy forest of pine,
tall, straight, with sunlight glancing through the crowns
as though celebrating the retreat of the sea millennia ago
but "we pass through as though feeling our way
at night in the hallways of an apartment
with glue-gun in hand, afraid of stepping
on an abandoned toy,
something like a vacuum-cleaner filter"
that's what this reminds me of, you announce
and I've got nothing to say
for a while we stand quietly by the stone with the photograph
until you find the right words once more
"And you know there was this time he and I were kissing
after a concert". What can you say after that?
"I can give you a lift back".
Drive the car in draw-n-out silence, that's all I'm good at.

МНЕМОНИЧЕСКОЕ ПРАВИЛО

Л.Л.

Не зря я все-таки ходил в свое время на курсы улучшения памяти.

Вот надо запомнить, когда у нее день рождения, просто составил предложение, в котором число букв каждого слова совпадает с соответствующей цифрой в дате, и готово.

Захотел потом поздравить ее на французском — использовал для фонетического запоминания, как учили, созвучные, пусть и далекие по смыслу, русские слова.

Чтобы лучше запомнилась книга, которую она подарила, по ходу чтения делал пометки на полях, и действительно помогло, а ведь я их потом даже не перечитывал.

Из названий парфюмов и имен модельеров, которых она упоминала чаще, сочинил песенку (есть и такой прием в мнемотехнике), чтобы напевать про себя, подыскивая ей подарок.

Когда уже жили вместе, список покупок никогда не записывал, а запоминал, составляя по методике остросюжетную историю, где ключевые роли играли нужные товары.

Или теперь вот хочется навсегда запомнить ту нашу поездку в Лиепаю – просто связал все яркими зрительными образами и расставил в уме на книжных полках, как фотографии.

Все планы, которые мы обсуждали на будущее, но так и не успели осуществить, зарифмовал списком, составив забавный стишок – теперь точно из головы никуда не денется.
А чтобы до утра не забылась фраза, которая должна обязательно ее вернуть, только сейчас не дает спать, можно не усложнять – просто держу рядом с кроватью блокнот и ручку.

Вообще, стал вести дневник, что-то вроде воспоминаний, чтобы наше с ней время не ускользало из неверной памяти, может даже книжка получиться или поэма.

Есть еще план как следует увековечить ее имя – собрать подписи за переименование улицы, все, конечно, будут думать, что это в честь ее исторической тезки, но я-то буду знать.

Лучше всего, конечно, было бы поставить где-нибудь в центре, на берегу канала, памятник тогда точно останется в памяти навсегда, но вот внешнего сходства, жаль, никакого...

Что же касается волос, неожиданно обнажающих ее плечи, или луны восходящей из-за ее бедра, тяжести ее груди в ладони, тепла нашей постели на выходных, вкуса долгих поцелуев бессонной ночью, запаха объятий за ненадобностью слов, вспыхивающего вдруг после долгого молчания голоса и других таких вот мучительных воспоминаний, – я и правда не знаю, как теперь все это забыть.

THE RULE OF MNEMONICS
To L. L.

It's a good thing all the same that I took a course to improve memory that time.

Needed to remember her birthday, and just made a sentence in which the number of letters in each word corresponded to the successive numbers in the date, and was golden.

Then wanted to wish her happy birthday in French, and for phonetic recall used Russian words of unrelated meaning that sounded similar, just like they taught.

In order to remember better the book she gave as a gift, made notes in the margins while reading, and it really did help, even though I never looked back at them later on.

From the names of perfumes and fashion designers that she mentioned most frequently I made up a little song (it's a mnemonic device); that I could sing to myself when looking for a present for her.

After we started living together I never wrote down a shopping list, memorizing it instead using the method of an exciting story in which the things we needed played key roles.

Or even now when I wanted to remember forever that trip we took to Liepaja, I just collected everything in intense visual images and set them out on bookshelves in my mind, like photographs.

I took all the plans that we made for the future but never actually realized and made a rhyming list, resulting in a funny little poem – now there's no way I'll ever forget that.

And in order not to forget by the morning the phrase that will absolutely bring her back and that won't let me sleep at the moment, there's a simple solution: keep a notepad and pen by the bedside.

In general, I started to keep a diary, something like reminiscences, so that our time together won't fade away from unreliable memory; maybe something like a book or a long poem will come of it.

There's also a plan to immortalize her memory for real – to collect signatures to rename a street; of course, everyone will think it's in honour of her historical namesake, but I'll know the truth.

It'd be even better to put up a monument in the centre, on the banks of the canal, and then she'd remain in memory forever, though unfortunately there's no physical resemblance between them...

But when it comes to her hair, when it unexpectedly bared her shoulders, or the moon appearing from behind her hips, her breast's weight in the hand, the warmth of our bed at weekends, the taste of long kisses on a sleepless night, the scent of embracing at the needlessness of words, the voice that resounded suddenly after a long silence, and all the other awful memories like that – I have no idea how to forget it all.

ШОССЕ

Если ты живешь в местечке
которое большинство проезжающих
считает досадной необходимостью
сбросить скорость
а сами проезжающие за день
превосходят числом
местное население в несколько раз
то тебе должно быть сразу ясно
насколько подозрительно выглядит
легковая машина в тени
припаркованная перед грузовиком
на узкой обочине тоннеля
проложенного транзитным потоком
в кронах деревьев…
что там под тентом
что за темными стеклами
второго ряда…
может и ничего такого
просто совпадение

HIGHWAY

If you live in a village
considered by most who drive through
just an annoying reason
to put on the brakes
and those who do pass by each day
exceed in number
the local population by several times over
then it should be immediately clear to you
how suspicious it is to see
a private car in the shadows
parked in front of a truck
on the narrow shoulder of the tunnel
cut by the freight traffic
through the crowns of the trees…
what's that under the canvas sheeting
what's behind the smoked windows
at the back…
maybe nothing at all
just a coincidence

* * *

Сквозь шелест земельных работ
до нашего поля долго доносится
прежде чем появиться на склоне шоссе
со стороны эстонской границы
сперва стремительной точкой
черный наездник прильнувший
в скульптурных одеждах и
угрожающе натягивающий
своим темным мотоциклом
пустой воскресный воздух
вглубь нашего края пока
по долям облегающего тела
к мотоциклу и длинным тонким
волосам из-под шлема
не узнаем хрупкую белую Лиину
отвечающую в таллинской библиотеке
за оцифровывание книг
после чего пейзаж разрешается
прорванный в точке отказа
ее исчезновением
а в восстановленной тишине
изъятого из земли металла
слышно что наша мысль на страже
даже не бросается вдогонку
нет, Лиина, сами мы верим лишь в то
что можно потрогать руками

Through the rustle of the earth works
it takes a long while to reach our field
before appearing on the incline of the highway
coming from the Estonian border
at first as a speeding point
a black rider clinging
in sculptural clothing and
threateningly pulling
with a dark motorcycle
empty Sunday air
deep into our locale until
by the lines of the body, wrapped
around the motorcycle and long, thin
hair from under the helmet
we recognize fragile pale Liina
responsible in the Tallinn library
for book digitization
then the scene comes into focus
pierced at the point of refusal
by her disappearance
and in the re-established quiet
in pursuit of that metal, pulled from the earth
we sense that our alert thought
cannot even begin to give chase
no, Liina, we ourselves believe only in
what we can touch with our hands.

ПОЛТОРОЙ ЭТАЖ

Потолок со скосами
так что выпрямиться
можно только посередине
но лечь места хватит всем
это все же лучше чем в палатке
крыша над головой
нагрелась за день так
что дышать нечем
а окна не открыть
заколочены
еще на прошлую зиму
комары тем не менее как-то пробрались
непонятно и все-таки
ты почему-то соглашаешься на этот вариант

PERFORMANCE: SOVIET RETRO DISCO

ONE-AND-A-HALFTH FLOOR

The ceiling slopes
so you can only stand up
in the middle
but there's room for everyone to lie down
all the same it's better than in a tent
the roof overhead
gets so hot in the day
you can't even breathe
and can't open windows
boarded up
for last winter
even so mosquitoes managed to get in
can't understand but anyhow
for some reason you decide on this option

ПОЕЗДКА В ГОРОД

В ответ с набранного наугад номера
приходит адрес одного из тех домов в центре
стеклянные купола над подъездами которых
пропускают внутрь дневной свет для освещения пролетов
а ночью светят обратно в небо над крышами

Введенный с ошибкой код все равно открывает
чужую квартиру уже обставленную впрочем твоими вещами
где незнакомые люди с одинаковым запахом геля для душа
обнимают тебя называя случайные имена
одно их верное движение и всякое желание пропадает

Забыв о краске на пальцах касаешься лица
и в зеркале видно как хорошо облегает мхом
твоя аккуратная седая борода
так что единственное возможное желание теперь

TRIP TO THE CITY

In the reply from the number chosen at random
you get the address of one of those houses in the centre
with glass cupolas over the entrance halls that
let in daylight for illumination of the stairwells
and at night shine light back out above the roofs

The code entered with an error all the same opens
the stranger's apartment, though it's already full of your stuff
where unknown people all smelling of the same shower gel
embrace you, calling you by arbitrary names
after just one correct gesture all desire disappears

Forgetting about the paint on your fingers you touch your face
and in the mirror see how well the moss covers
your neat silvery beard
so that the single desire that is now possible
is to stay like this as long as possible – for many more years

* * *

Сегодня я понял
что еще никогда в жизни
не набирал слово лодыжка
ни записывать от руки
ни разу насколько я помню
не приходилось
как так могло получиться
лодыжка лодыжка лодыжка
много ли еще таких слов
как узнать
набираешь ты мне каждый знак
или просто копируешь свое
прощай прощай прощай прощай

INSTALLATION: OBJECT NO. 4

Today I understood
that I have never yet in my life
typed the word anklebone
and I've never had occasion
to write it longhand either
as far as I can recall
how could that be
anklebone anklebone anklebone
are there many other words like that
how can one know
are you typing out every character to me
or just copying your
goodbye goodbye goodbye goodbye
goodbye goodbye goodbye goodbye

НЕ СЕЗОН

Объем, вытесненный в общем пейзаже
зданием сельской церкви, равен
Тому дню, когда мы за ненадобностью
отдали знакомым детское сидение
Дню, когда я понял, что звуки рассохшегося органа
больше не возносят мой дух
Зато среди низкорослого леса
на торфяных топях, могу долго
отрешенно наблюдать,
как сапоги понемногу теснят дно.

INSTALLATION: OBJECT NO. 5

WRONG SEASON

The volume displaced in the overall landscape
by the building of the village church, is equal to
the day that we gave away to acquaintances
that child's seat we didn't need any longer
the day I grasped that the sounds of the desiccated organ
no longer elevate my spirit
in the peat bog I can inertly
observe for a long while
Although in the scrub forest
how boots slowly displace the land

ТРЕБУЮТСЯ

Программист-разработчик
Бухгалтер-делопроизводитель
Руководитель проектов
Сертифицированный землемер
Автослесарь грузового транспорта
Установщик душевых кабин
Продавец-консультант
Переводчик со шведского...
Все они востребованы
Даже специалист по физике звука
может иногда найти у нас
работу по специальности...
Я же самостоятельно даже вес тела
в момент удара о землю
после падения с моего балкона
рассчитать не сумею
Читал тоже не то чтобы много
И то почти ничего не запомнилось...
Нет, Андерса Петерсена тоже не знаю
А-а-а, работы вроде видел
Но имени тогда не запомнил

NOW HIRING

A programmer-developer
Accountant-record keeper
Project manager
Certified land surveyor
Mechanic for freight trucks
Shower installer
Salesman-consultant
Translator from Swedish...
All are wanted
Even a specialist in acoustic physics
Can at times find
Appropriate employment here...
Without help, even the weight of a body
At the moment of impact with the ground
After falling from my balcony
I wouldn't be able to calculate
And I can't say that I've read a lot
And remember practically nothing of that...
No, I also don't know Anders Petersen
Oh, right, I guess I've seen the works
But I didn't remember the name

* * *

Она хорошо подготовилась:
рассталась со своим парнем ушла с работы
сдала взятую в кредит квартиру продала машину
раздала подругам вещи
и карточки скидок
перегнала всю музыку в mp3
удалила профиль и старые письма
купила новый лаптоп
навестила бабушку и теток
научила маму писать SMS
помирилась с младшей сестрой
перестала есть мясо, читать новости
вернула наконец в библиотеку ноты
подписалась на несколько дельных рассылок.
Надписью «Берлин» остановила фуру
и за всю Польшу не произнесла ни слова…
И теперь, несколько съемных квартир спустя
засыпая одна в комнате со стенами
выкрашенными прошлыми жильцами в белый
она вглядывается в темный воздух, где
отчетливо ощущается чье-то незримое присутствие
она прислушивается к себе – вот бы знать наверняка
что теперь это с ней по-настоящему
все уже так, как надо

She prepared well:
broke up with her boyfriend
quit her job
rented out the apartment she bought with loans
sold her car
gave her girlfriends all her stuff
and her discount cards
transferred all her music to mp3s
deleted her profile and her old mail
bought a new laptop
visited her grandmother and aunts
taught her mother how to text
made peace with her younger sister
stopped eating meat, reading the news
finally returned her sheet music to the library
signed up for some useful LISTSERVS.
Waved down a truck with her "Berlin" sign
and didn't say a single word through all of Poland….
And now, several rented apartments later
falling asleep alone in a room with walls
painted white by the previous tenants
she peers into the dark air, where
someone's invisible presence can be clearly felt
she listens to herself – if only she could know for sure
that now this is really it,
now everything is how it should be.

* * *

Странные вещи бывают порой прикреплены
к оконным рамам фасадных домов,
ладно, кормушка, а то зеркало заднего вида,
даже целых два, корзинка или, представьте,
ржавый колокольчик – в окне четвертого этажа.
Я верю, всему есть свое объяснение,
так, буквально несколькими жестами удалось установить,
что этот парень приехал к нам из Пярну,
а эта девушка, например, полностью вышла из газеты
и впредь будет сидеть за кассовым аппаратом,
и все только потому, что на нем меньше клавиш...
Стоит ли и дальше прикидываться простым прохожим?
Сколько можно коситься на крыши,
шарахаться срывающихся капель?
Кому и зачем может понадобиться колокольчик
(вариант: зеркало заднего вида) в окне последнего этажа?
Что здесь делают люди из твоего прошлого?
На чей счет принимать их легкие улыбки?
Кто в твое отсутствие позаботится,
чтобы баночки на кухне были полны: чай, кофе, сахар?
Что еще? В своей объяснительной
дать краткие ответы в удобной форме.

* * *

Куда завел по ключевому слову поиск
по собственному имени, преследуя по ссылкам,
вдруг обнаружишь двадцать лет спустя
себя в квартире без единой книги,
без книжных полок.
Твой городок совсем осел, и никогда
(ты можешь досмотреть прогноз погоды до конца)
и никогда ни на одном канале
твой городок синоптиком не будет упомянут.
(Погода выпадает наугад.)
Зато натоплено по-стариковски, что зубы портятся,
что по-старушечьи готовят, морковкой мелкою
(с лотка торгуешь пока свет) немытою
распались сонно пальцы – пульт падает
пульт падает, и пульт упал на пол... Простыл,
в простых запутаешься простынях, проспишь, разбудят
(затравленный счетами, шумит сосед за каждою стеной),
спросонок взгляд на обоях соберешь, на этом снимке
к тебе еще не применен утюг уюта,
еще кредитом неподъемным держится ваш брак
еще в рассрочку дом, еще – компьютер
чувствительнее к перепадам тока,
чем ты – давления, как вдруг спохватишься,
в последний день недели отключат сеть,
пойдешь пройтись, активные все окна
попробуешь закрыть, попросишь книг,
хотя бы тех – для бедных: сто
    способов разбогатеть,
    исправить карму, десять шагов к
    ответам, ...,
как выйти замуж, похудеть…
Как мне отсюда выйти?

Where were you led by the keyword search
for your own name, following the links,
you suddenly find yourself twenty years later
in an apartment without a single book,
without bookshelves.
Your town has completely gone to seed, and never
(you can watch the weather forecast to the end)
never on a single channel
will the meteorologist mention it.
(Weather takes shape at random)
Yet the heating is set old-man high, which ruins teeth,
and cooking like old ladies, like unwashed carrot runts
(you work a market stall until dark) sleepily
your fingers part – the remote falls
the remote falls and the remote fell to the floor…. Caught a cold,
you get tangled up in plain sheets, oversleep, are roused
(tormented by bills, a neighbour rages through every wall),
you throw a questioning glance at wallpaper, in this shot
you've not yet been subjected to the iron of domesticity,
your marriage is still supported by overwhelming credit,
the house is still mortgaged, and still – the computer
is more sensitive to spikes in the current than you
to shifts in pressure, and suddenly you come to your senses,
on the last day of the week they shut down the network,
you take a stroll, try to shut
all active window, ask for books,
at the least the ones for poor folk: one hundred ways to get rich,
to repair karma, answers in ten steps, …
how to get married, lose weight…
How can I get out of here?

* * *

Предплюсна, плюсна, фаланги пальцев
Предплюсна, плюсна, фаланги пальцев.
Надев темные очки, повторяй эти слова.
За очками чудится какая-то глубина,
но высказать ее нельзя
за словами чудится какая-то глубина,
но высказать ее нельзя
в поэтах наблюдается какая-то глубина
какая-то пустота какая-то пустота какая-то пустота.
Предплюсна, плюсна, фаланги пальцев –
это поэзия, это стихи

PERFORMANCE: PUNTE AT MALA

Metatarsal, tarsal, phalanges of the digits
Metatarsal, tarsal, phalanges of the digits.
Put on dark glasses and repeat these words.
Beyond the lenses gleams a kind of depth,
but it can't be said aloud
beyond the words gleams a kind of depth,
but it can't be said aloud
in poets there appears a kind of depth
a kind of void a kind of void a kind of void
Metatarsal, tarsal, phalanges of the digits –
this is poetry, this is verse.

ГОД ВРЕМЕНИ

август
все что я могу сделать сегодня вечером
припарковать рядом с твоим домом
этот свой пыльный фургон с надписью
фрукты тропических стран
и пообещать что утром до работы
мы обязательно съездим к морю
пока стоит такая погода
но ведь все равно получится что проспим...
говорят окраины сгорят вместе с летом

октябрь
и тогда дерево в нашем дворе – это каштан –
опаленным краем десятого месяца
срежет к чертям городскую башню
на что есть верная примета:
видишь листья который день
показывают обратную сторону
дереву сделать такое труднее

январь
чем заложнику подать беспомощный знак
в стране где к ним
никогда не приходят на помощь
чтобы не создавать прецедент
понимаешь обугленные зазубрины
обугленные зазубрины
всю зиму в окне

апрель
вот что будет потом..
но пока день освещает
две грани любого дома
открою тебе причину своей
    печали:
этой весной с живого друга
    гипсовую снял маску
за что похоже наказан

A YEAR'S TIME

August
all I can do this evening
is pull in next to your building and park
this dusty van of mine with the words
tropical fruits on the side
and promise that before work in the morning
we'll definitely drive out to the beach
while the weather's this nice
but all the same it'll turn out we overslept...
they say the outskirts will burn up along with
    summer

October
and then the tree in our yard – the chestnut –
will get pruned by the tenth month's singed edge
into the shape of the city tower,
as you can tell by a sure sign:
see, for days its leaves have been
turned inside out
it's harder for a tree to do that

January
than it is to signal helplessness to a hostage
in a country where no one
ever comes to their aid
in order not to set precedents
you understand charred stumps
charred stumps
out the window all winter

April
that's what there'll be...
but for the time being the day illuminates
two sides of every building
I'll reveal the secret of my sadness to you:
this spring I made a plaster mask
from a living friend's face
for which I'm being punished it seems

* * *

Как-то полюбила меня девушка с улицы Джохара Дудаева
я ее избегал много работал и всегда мог сослаться на занятость

потом я все-таки пригляделся к девушке с улицы Джохара Дудаева
мы поладили и я много работал вдохновленный нашей любовью

но долго так продолжаться не могло бросил я девушку с улицы Джохара Дудаева
стал много работать чтобы она больше не докучала мне своей любовью

нет думаю нехорошо это надо вернуть девушку с улицы Джохара Дудаева
но она уже нашла другого пришлось много работать чтобы как-то забыть ее

теперь вроде собираются переименовать эту улицу и тогда наверное
все встанет на свои места и можно будет спокойно заняться своими делами.

BIOGRAPHICAL NOTES

SEMYON KHANIN is an artist and poet writing in Russian, a translator of Latvian poetry into Russian, editor of numerous poetry collections of Russian and Latvian poets. He is the compiler of the anthology *Latvian / Russian Poetry. Poems in Russian written by Latvian Poets*. Books of Khanin's poems have been published in Latvian, Czech, Ukrainian, Serbian, and Italian. His poems in English translation have been published in *Poetry Wales*, *Brooklin Rail* and *Artful Dodge*. He is an author of *Just Now* (2003), *Missed Details* (2008) and *Afloat* (2013). His selected poems were published in 2017 under the title *But Not With That*. Khanin also makes his own performances and installations (single-face theatre, three-dimensional poetry etc.).

ARTŪRS PUNTE (b. 1977) is a poet, editor and multimedia artist. He has edited numerous poetry collections, and together with Alexander Zapol he has been an editor of the anthology *Contemporary Russian Poetry in Latvia: 1985-2005*. Punte's poems have been translated into English, German and other languages. He lives in Riga and writes in Russian and Latvian. He is one of the founders of ORBITA.

SERGEY TIMOFEYEV (b. 1970) is a poet, journalist, translator, and DJ. He is the author of seven poetry collections. His poems are translated into English, Italian, Swedish, German, Ukrainian, and other languages, and he actively participates in poetry festivals around the world. He was one of the first in the post-soviet cultural space to invent the genre of poetry-video and his first video-poetry work *Orchestra Rehearsal* was made in 1994  in collaboration with the filmmaker Victor Vilx. He is one of the founders of ORBITA. Sergey Timofeyev lives in Riga and writes in Russian, continuing to mix modern poetry with other art-forms and media.

VLADIMIR SVETLOV (b. 1973) is a poet, photographer, and performer. His poetry has been translated into Latvian, English, German, and Italian. He is one of the participants of the multimedia poetry project ORBITA. His first book of poems in Russian and Latvian was published in 2014, along with his photographs.

PHOTOS: TOMS HARJO

KEVIN M. F. PLATT is a professor of Russian and East European Studies at the University of Pennsylvania, USA. He has published translations of many Russian poets, including those included in this volume, as well as Shamshad Abdullaev, Keti Chukhrov, Dmitry Golynko, Osip Mandelstam, Fedor Swarovski, and others. His latest book project is the edited collection of scholarly essays *Global Russian Cultures*, forthcoming from the University of Wisconsin Press.

PHOTO: AUTHOR'S ARCHIVE

www.ingramcontent.com/pod-product-compliance
Lightning Source LLC
Chambersburg PA
CBHW041927090426
42743CB00021B/3462